LEAVES
FROM A
PEASANT'S COTTAGE DRAWER

Plaque carved by Natasha Smith.
Photograph by kind permission of James MacGregor.

Matador
9 De Montfort Mews
Leicester LE1 7FW, UK
Tel: (+44) 116 255 9311 / 9312
Email: books@troubador.co.uk
Web: www.troubador.co.uk/matador

ISBN 978-1906510-565

Cover image: © Photos.com

Typeset in 11pt Bembo by Troubador Publishing Ltd, Leicester, UK

Matador is an imprint of Troubador Publishing Ltd

LEAVES

FROM A

PEASANT'S COTTAGE DRAWER

J. HOGG, PRINTER, EDINBURGH

TO

THE WORKING MEN OF THE BORDER

THESE POEMS ARE CHIEFLY DEDICATED

————————

AS I AM ACQUAINTED CHIEFLY WITH THE SCENES WITH WHICH

THE COTTAGE ABOUNDS,

AND AM PERSUADED THAT IT CONTAINS

THE VERY SOUL AND LIFE-BLOOD OF OUR COUNTRY

MORE TRUE WORTH OF THE PLEASURES OF THE HEART BEING

FOUND AROUND ITS SIMPLE HEARTH

THAT IN MANY A STATELIER DWELLING

I FEEL THAT, WHILST YOU ARE WORTHY OF A FAR

NOBLER MUSE THAN MINE,

I CAN HAVE NO MORE NOBLE PATRON THAN YOURSELVES

THE WORKING MEN OF THE BORDER.

LEAVES

FROM A

PEASANT'S COTTAGE DRAWER:

BEING

POEMS BY ROBERT DAVIDSON,

DAY-LABOURER, MOREBATTLE, ROXBURGHSHIRE.

"There is a pleasure in poetic pain,
Which only poets know" Cowper.

Edinburgh:
Published by James Hogg, 122 Nicolson Street.
MDCCCXLVIII

CONTENTS

—∿∿—

Notes

Addenda

ACKNOWLEDGEMENTS

The Robert Davidson Memorial Committee wishes to thank the following individuals and organisations for their generous financial support. This republication would not have been possible without their help.

The Kelso Arts Appreciation Society

The Jinty Scott Memorial Fund
Kalewater Community Council

Barbara Lucas of Latham, New York State, USA
The Duke of Roxburghe.
The Hon Robert Loder
The Dick Family.
Matilda Mitchell
Mrs Alison Salvesen
Mrs Jean Jones
Penelope Holland in memory of Mervyn Pike.

The Committee also wishes to thank several anonymous donors and the 136 people who sponsored pages. Their financial support has been invaluable but the names are too numerous to receive individual mention here.

ROBERT DAVIDSON: AN INTRODUCTION

—◦◦◦—

We know little about the life of Robert Davidson, 'The Morebattle Poet'. Although the anonymous author(s) of *The History of Morebattle and District* (1966) shows a first hand familiarity with Davidson's poems, no living tradition about his life and work appears otherwise to have survived in the locality.[1] What we do know derives primarily from the short autobiography with which Davidson prefaced his third and final collection of poems *Leaves From A Peasant's Cottage Drawer* (1848).[2]

Though brief, Davidson's account of his life is unusual and valuable. This is because in his time very few people who undertook hard physical labour for their livelihood ever managed to write down for posterity their own accounts of their lives. History does not normally speak to us through the writings of people like Robert Davidson – people who lived their lives in poverty and often on the edge of utter destitution and who, like Davidson, ended their days as recipients of parish relief.[3] Normally, we hear about people in such circumstances only when they get spoken for by others. And so, if their point of view ever gets heard at all, it gets heard only indirectly and indistinctly. We are fortunate therefore that we have Davidson to tell us his thoughts about the times in which he lived and, since he is an accomplished poet, to tell us about his *feelings* for the people and the places in the district that he loved.

Davidson wrote his autobiography in 1847, "his seventieth year".[4] In it he tells us that having begun his working life as a cowherd, he then became a ploughman, then a "day-labourer", then again a ploughman and finally a "day–labourer" once more – the occupation which he "greatly preferred". It is perhaps worth exploring in a little detail what it meant to live a life like Davidson's, what it meant to undertake these different forms of employment and why Davidson changed between them in the way that he did. This may help us understand better both the context and the content of his poems.

As a ploughman or *hind* in the Roxburghshire of his day, Davidson's contract of employment would have been based on the 'Boll Wage'. That is, much the greater part of his wages would have been paid yearly and 'in kind'. In the 1840s, the value of his wage would have been approximately £25.8 *per annum* but only about 20% of this (about £5) would have been paid in ready cash. The rest was paid in oatmeal (10 or 12 bolls), barley (3 or 4 bolls) and peas or beans (1 or 2 bolls) – a 'Kelso Boll' being 6 bushels in weight. In addition, the hind got between 600 & 1700 yards of free, manured potato ground, free carriage of up to 4 tons of coal, the keep of a cow and a 'free' cottage in return for 18 or 20 days labour from a female worker or *bondager*. Other traditional elements in this yearly contract – enough ground to sow a capful of lint or flax seed, ground to keep chickens, knife-sharpening corn, 'sheep siller' etc were commuted to cash payments at various points in time.

By contrast, the agricultural "day-labourer" was paid a weekly wage in cash. This is probably what attracted Davidson – liberty being a key theme in several of his poems. Employment as a "day-labourer" gave him much greater freedom to dispose of his income as he wished. In good years & seasons, the real value of the hind & day-labourer's wages were more or less the same (the day-labourer earning perhaps slightly more than the hind) but the day-labourer could spend (or save) his income exactly as he pleased. In ill years & seasons, however, the greater security of the hind's wages 'in kind' asserted itself – and so we see Davidson reverting to this mode of employment in the bad years following 1811.

Of course, the balance of advantages and disadvantages here were marginal and the facts of life for people in Davidson's circumstances could be extremely brutal indeed. A short period out of work of a few weeks or months because of injury or illness or for whatever reason could quickly wipe out the careful savings of years, visiting catastrophe upon the families of even the most sober, thrifty and industrious workmen.

It is not for nothing that from time to time Davidson describes Scotland as *"The Land o' Cakes"* – i.e. the land of *oatcakes* - in his poems. The diet of agricultural workers like him was monotonous and poor. It was almost always porridge or potatoes (though not necessarily always in that order) morning, noon and night. As the *Report of the Royal Commission on Lunatic Asylums* of 1857 states:

> In the rural districts of the Lowlands, oatmeal and potatoes consti-
> tute the chief part of the diet of the peasantry, with the addition of
> milk and garden vegetables. Bread is occasionally used, but butcher-
> meat very seldom forms part of the living.

According to this same *Report,* those from amongst the very poorest in rural society, the aged and infirm of body or of mind, those who could not per-form hard physical work and who had no one to support them subsisted, in so far as they were able to get them, more or less exclusively upon potatoes. This was a starvation diet at the best of times and the failure of the potato crop from blight in the years 1846-57 must have caused considerable priva-tion and distress not only in Ireland and in the Highlands but also in such rel-atively prosperous agricultural districts as the Borders. It may well have been to something like this diet that Davidson was reduced when living in his declining years with his daughter Christian, his son in law George Smith, their nine children and two others in the shepherd's cottage at Upper Chatto.

In Davidson's time, housing and sanitation were simply awful for the vast majority of people living in Scotland. *The Report of the Royal Commission on the Poor Law (Scotland)* of 1844 described a typical hind's cottage in Roxburghshire as follows:

> Of one apartment with a little porch inside, divided by the box beds
> into two areas, one for living and one for storing lumber: it had no
> ceiling but matting laid over the rafters.

As late as 1893, *The Report on the Agricultural Labourer, Scotland (Roxburghshire & Berwickshire)* stated that:

> Privies are conspicuous by their absence or, if present, by their non-
> use for the purposes for which they were intended. Here again, old
> habits die hard, but men so very often complain now of the want of
> them, and say they consider there ought to be one to each house.

With dire living conditions such as these it is not surprising to find

Davidson writing poems on such themes as the *Visitation of the Cholera* or to find that many of his poems – *Churchyard Musings, On Visiting the Grave of a Young Friend, A Mother's Lament for the Death of an Infant Son, Epitaphs* – are reflections upon untimely death and loss.

We catch a glimpse of Davidson living at Morebattle in the 1841 Census of the parish. It is not possible, from the way the Census was taken, to determine exactly where he lived in the village. From the Census information as presented, the best guess is that he was living somewhere in the little lane off Teapot Street that runs behind and parallel to Main Street. There is no reason to suppose that the cottages there or anywhere else in the village were very much better than those available to hinds on the farms. In Morebattle house number 20 on the Census we find the following inhabitants: John Oliver (Mason); his wife Agnes; his aged mother Mary and his four young children; William Melrose (Carrier) and his wife Janet; Jacob Entwisle (Tailor), his wife Sophia and infant son Jonathan; Robert Davidson (Day-Labourer), his wife Christian and their son Robert – a total of three families and sixteen people of all ages in a cottage which may have been little more than a 'but and ben'. With overcrowding like this, it is a wonder that Davidson ever found himself alone with his thoughts long enough even simply to write them down.

Given the much-vaunted qualities of a traditional Scottish education, it is interesting that in his autobiography Davidson describes his late eighteenth century schooling as being "paltry". More interesting still is his account of how the meagre ration afforded him was supplemented. The auld wives spinning yarn and telling the local children the Border tales by their firesides, the kindly farmer allowing Davidson free range of the books and newspapers of what was presumably a subscription "country library" provided our poet with a window upon the world which the dominie at his local school could not.[5]

Given the apparently low educational standards in the village of his day, it is perhaps surprising therefore that, as Davidson says, "very few cottages were without Boston's and Erskine's works". Few modern readers will have the stamina, the philosophical or theological training to make much sense of books like Thomas Boston's *Human Nature in its Fourfold Estate* (1720). And yet here we see the long dissenting tradition of the Scottish Church being sustained not only by the *spoken* word, by the exhortations and sermons of its charismatic preachers, but also by a people thoroughly familiar with the *written* word in which the great theological questions of the day were being discussed. What today now seem to us bafflingly obscure points of religious doctrine once divided Scottish communities to the point of violence – as Davidson's poem *The Ordination* shows – and Morebattle was ever in the thick of it. The Halls of nearby Haughhead and the Bennets of Grubet & Marlefield were amongst the leading Scottish Covenanting families of the seventeenth century. The Gateshaw Brae gatherings of the eighteenth century sustained this vigorous dissenting tradition in the locality. In Davidson's day and for a long time beforehand, Morebattle was a place in which people took their religion extremely seriously. Not only were the people willing to *fight* for their religion, they were also more than willing to expend considerable effort *reading* about it as well.[6]

In his autobiography, Davidson mentions no literary influences other than the national poet himself, Robert Burns, of whom Davidson says he had never heard until some "two years after his death" (i.e. not until 1798 when Davidson was already twenty years of age) and 'Blind Harry' whose story in verse of the *Life of Sir William Wallace* was once said to have been the most popular book in Scotland after the Bible. Ben Jonson (1572-1637) is however quoted at the end of Davidson's autobiography and Oliver Goldsmith (1730–1774) is admired as a "great poet".[7]

It is perhaps not too difficult to see the influence of a poem like Goldsmith's famous *The Deserted Village* in Davidson's *On Visiting the Scenes of Bygone Days* and to this extent it may be said that Davidson's poetic talent is the product of much careful study of past masters in the arts of versifying just as much as it is the result of many long years of practice in these same arts. Other clues in the autobiography hint at this. Davidson tells us that he was composing poems in his head from an early age and while labouring at the plough but that he never wrote any of his poems down until after he was married. He tells us that he destroyed all his manuscripts not once but twice. Everything in Davidson's autobiography suggests a writer consciously trying to live up to the highest possible standards. We are not looking at the work of an uneducated man here. We are looking at a man who was self-educated to a very high standard – and who carefully measured his work against the very best that he knew.

What else may be gleaned from Davidson's autobiography? He tells us that at the age of ten (i.e. in 1788) he was herding cows because "the country was then almost unenclosed". The Old and New Statistical Accounts of the relevant parishes would seem to suggest that this date for enclosure is rather late, the agricultural revolution and the fencing in of the traditional open fields being already under way for a decade and more in the Borders. As the reader will discover, many of Davidson's poems reflect the social tensions which this huge set of changes caused in the rural life of Scotland. The fact that, like many others, Davidson's family did not prosper from these changes – and may indeed have been seriously disadvantaged by them - makes his point of view informative and important. The reader of the poems will see how well Davidson weighs and balances his judgments upon the matters in question. While several of Davidson's poems refer approvingly to certain landlords, clergymen and others in similar positions, the Dedication which Davidson wrote to accompany *Leaves* – "To the Working Men of the Border" - shows us where his sympathies broadly lay. His view of life is perhaps best summed up in his *Epistle to William Bennet:*

> *The means of human happiness*
> *Are very equal shared;*
> *For when we right consider a',*
> *We find the distance is but sma',*
> *'Tween cottars and the laird.*

What do we know of Davidson's reputation? Davidson received a short accolade from Alexander Jeffrey in volume iv of his *History & Antiquities of Roxburghshire* (1864) pp. 370-1:

> Apart from his poems, his life presents one of the finest specimens of a genuine true-hearted Scottish peasant. His verses are marked with a good deal of humour and occasionally by felicity of expression worthy of a higher master of the art of rhyme. The moral sentiments of his graver pieces are of the happiest kind.

Sir George Douglas makes a passing reference to "the idyllic strains of Robert Davidson" in his *History of the Border Counties of Roxburghshire, Selkirkshire & Peeblesshire* (1896) p.428. Again, James Tait in volume one of his *Two Centuries of Border Church Life* (1889) pp.136-7 makes mention of one of Davidson's poems - *The Ordination* – a poem which humorously describes the riot that accompanied the induction of the Reverend James

Christie to Morebattle Church in 1725. (Tait here also mentions the fact that Davidson was for a time a member of the Secession Church in Morebattle). Finally, the Reverend Charles Rogers in *The Scottish Minstrel* (1885) p.245 adds some approbatory notes to the life and work of Davidson:

> Many of his poems are powerful both in expression and sentiment. In private life he was sober, prudent and industrious.

As for the rest, "there is nought but the silent condescension of history". Professor William Veitch's *History and Poetry of the Scottish Border* (1878) – an otherwise admirably well-informed and comprehensive collection – says nothing. The Reverend W. S Crockett's *Berwickshire and Roxburghshire* (1926) contains a *Roll of Honour* chapter which includes the names of a number of Border poets but which omits Davidson. Given that Crockett had previously published a poetry collection entitled *Minstrelsy of the Merse: the Poets and Poetry of Berwickshire* in 1893, a volume which demonstrates the author's close familiarity with the subject of Border poets, this oversight by an otherwise learned and careful scholar suggests that Davidson's name fell quickly into obscurity. This is a judgement confirmed by the recent publication of Walter Elliot's *New Border Minstrelsy* (2006). When in the Scottish Borders the peerless and indefatigable Walter Elliot disnae mind your name, you really have been forgotten!

What has subsequent research discovered about Davidson? We can now confirm that, as both Jeffrey and Rogers (op. cit.) noted, Robert Davidson was born at Lempitlaw in the parish of Sprouston in the year 1778.[8] His father, Robert Davidson, was an 'indweller' at Lempitlaw. His mother's maiden name was Janet Stirling.

Robert the poet was the eldest of five brothers and one sister: William, James, Henry, Richard and Isabel. William joined the Royal Navy. He was with Nelson at the Battle of the Nile. He lost his leg in an engagement off the Spanish coast, was pensioned off and became a revenue collector at Malta. He died while returning to Scotland to end his days and is buried at Kelso. James became a trumpeter in a cavalry regiment. His horse's head was shot off by a cannonball at Waterloo, severely injuring him in the face. Eventually retiring from the army, James lived at Kelso. Both William and James were cited for bravery. Richard emigrated to Canada.[9] The strongly patriotic and military themes of such Davidson poems as *Anna & Malcolm, The Laurels of Scotland* and *The Mountains of Spain* may well be informed by the experience of Robert's brothers in the service of their country.

Robert the poet married Christian Richardson. They had seven children: Robert (b. 1800); Janet (b.1802); James (b.1806); Isabella (b.1809); Christian (b.1811); William (b. 1813) and John (b 1817). John died in infancy in 1818. Isabella died aged 10 in 1819. It would be Robert, James and William therefore who were the three sons whom Davidson mentions in his autobiography as having emigrated to America.

Rogers (op. cit.) states that Robert the poet died in Hounam Parish in 1855 (exactly where he does not say). The Census of Hounam Parish for 1851 supports this contention. It records Robert Davidson, 'labourer', living with his daughter Christian and his son in law George Smith, 'shepherd', at Upper Chatto. Hounam churchyard contains the still legible gravestone of this Smith family. It lists a son of George and Christian, one John Smith, whom it says "died at Fly Creek Otsigo Co. N. America 7.7.1888".[10] Reasoning that this John Smith, a grandson of the poet, just might have gone to join his uncles Robert, James or William who were already settled in America, the search for Davidson's sons and their descendants consequently focussed upon this Otsego County (which upon enquiry was located in New York State, USA).

And there Davidson's descendants were found. The Davidson family historian Barbara Lucas still lives nearby at Latham in New York State. She has been able to confirm many of the details in this introduction and has added very considerably to our understanding of the family. Many of the poet's descendants have distinguished themselves in their choice of careers. Two have served their adopted country with great distinction.

Captain Andrew Davidson, son of James Davidson (b.1806) and grandson of the poet was born at Morebattle on 12 February 1840 and went to the USA with his family in 1846. Whilst a First Lieutenant, he served with the 30th U.S. Colored Troops – one of the first black regiments in the Union army. He won the Congressional Medal of Honor for gallantry at the Battle of the Mine, Petersburg, July 1864 (an action recreated in the opening scenes of the 2003 Hollywood movie *Cold Mountain*). Rear Admiral Walter Bunn Davidson (1901–1971) likewise distinguished himself in combat with the Legion of Merit "for outstanding services during operations against the enemy in the Western Pacific". Amongst his other appointments, he was for a time Commander of the USN Subic Bay Naval Base in the Philippines. (Information lately received from Barbara Lucas identifies John Robson, Premier of the Canadian Province of British Columbia (1889-1892), as a nephew of the poet).

Alexander Jeffrey concludes his entry on Robert Davidson in his *History & Antiquities of Roxburghshire* by saying that "it is not creditable to the admirers of peasant literature that no memorial marks the resting place of one who was an honour to his class and to the district in which he lived".[11] With the raising of a plaque on Morebattle churchyard wall to Davidson's memory and the republication of his *Leaves from a Peasant's Cottage Drawer* it is to be hoped that this deficiency has now been remedied.

David Welsh   2008

The endnotes immediately below refer to the above introduction. The explanatory notes following the poems themselves and the asterisked ★ notes in the text belong to the original edition of *Leaves*.

Endnotes

1. Information from Davidson Memorial Committee member Eileen Woodward strongly suggests that the individuals associated with this publication who were most likely to have been aware of Davidson and his work were Mr & Mrs Alec & Marie Mackie of Linton Schoolhouse. Mr Mackie taught history at Kelso High School and Mrs Mackie taught English. Both taught the author of this present introduction.

2. Although Davidson states in his autobiography that his second volume *Poems* was published in 1824, it was in fact printed at Jedburgh "for the author" by the well-known firm of W. Easton in 1825. Surviving copies of Davidson's books are now extremely rare – which is of course a very good reason for this republication. No copies of the 1811 edition of his poems appear to have survived anywhere. The National Library of Scotland has a copy of both the 1825 *Poems* and the 1848 *Leaves* editions. Only two other copies of the 1825 *Poems* are known to survive – in university libraries in the USA. Edinburgh, Glasgow, Aberdeen & Newcastle University Libraries each has a single copy

of *Leaves*. So has Scottish Borders Regional Archive. Another six copies of *Leaves* are held by university libraries in the United States. The Davidson Committee would be grateful for any information concerning other surviving copies.

3. "He was often oppressed by poverty; and, latterly, was the recipient of parochial relief ", C. Rogers, *Scottish Minstrel* (1885), p.244.

4. Alexander Somerville (1811-1885) of Berwickshire is sometimes said to have been the first working man anywhere to have published his autobiography – *Autobiography of a Working Man by One Who Has Whistled at The Plough* (1848) Somerville's book was in fact published in the same year Davidson published *Leaves* – which would make Davidson's reflections upon his life equally early. John Younger (1785–1860) of St Boswells, another vigorously opinionated working man from the Borders and a well-known writer and authority on angling, had his autobiography published some thirty or so years later in 1882 – *Autobiography of John Younger, Shoemaker, St Boswells* (though the period this describes (1785-1860) coincides to a large extent with that described by Davidson and so Younger supplies us with much useful material for comparison). 'Celery' Taylor (1803-1891) of Hounam Grange wrote a quite extraordinarily detailed account of his life in 1885 describing his early days in the Morebattle district (a period which again coincides to a large extent with the life of Davidson) before emigrating to the USA where, by introducing celery-growing to Kalamazoo (afterwards a major industry of that region), he acquired his nickname. This autobiography has never been published but is available on the internet (with many grievous spelling errors of place names to test the local knowledge of the reader) at: http://www.rootsweb.com/~mikalama/celerytaylor01.htm

5. Papers in the possession of Mr Neil Patterson of Morebattle show a Robert Davidson as having been a founder-member of the Morebattle Library at some point before the year 1824. A love of books and learning, acquired by Robert at an early age, was perhaps being passed on here.

6. Popular disturbances in Lowland Scotland in the late eighteenth and early nineteenth centuries were focused less upon such religious questions and more upon the kinds of everyday concerns which remain recognisable today. The tollgate riots in 1792 which were a protest against the introduction of road use charges (and which involved smashing and burning the gates on the new Berwickshire turnpikes at Duns, Paxton and Greenlaw) and the Kelso Bridge tollgate riot of 1854 are good examples. So were the anti-Militia riots which took place throughout Scotland and which caused acute anxiety in Government circles (comparisons being drawn with the ominous develop-

ments in revolutionary France).These disturbances began at Eccles in Berwickshire on 17 August 1797. Similar riots then took place at Lauder, Selkirk, Jedburgh and elsewhere in Scotland and they ended with twelve people being sabred and shot dead by the authorities at Tranent on 29 August, 1797 (one more than the number traditionally thought to have been killed at the better-known 'Peterloo Massacre' in Manchester, 1819). We can only imagine what the impact of such events might have been upon communities like Morebattle.

The *Roxburghshire Lieutenancy Book* of 1801 lists all those balloted into the Militia parish by parish (membership was decided by lot and the riots were directed principally against the parish schoolmasters whose task it was to keep lists of those chosen in the ballot and who had consequently been enrolled or conscripted into what was, in effect, a form of compulsory military service). Linton Parish lists a Robert Davidson 'Hind' working for a Mr Purves of Linton Burnfoot. No other Robert Davidson is listed in this or other nearby parishes and so, while it is possible that our Robert may have escaped the ballot altogether, this particular Militiaman may very well have been our poet.

These were the Militiamen who, once popular objections to their being raised had been overcome, took part in the famous 'False Alarm' of January 31, 1804 when the watch at Hume Castle mistook some heather burning on the moors near Scremerston for the signal of Napoleon's invasion, set light to their own beacon and consequently raised the whole fighting men of the Border to arms. Sir Walter Scott gives us a fictionalised and characteristically good-humoured and stirring account of this event in *The Antiquary* (1816).Younger (see above) gives a more jaundiced and near-seditious version as seen from the point of view of one who served in the rank and file and who actually participated in the event.

7. Several of Davidson's poems such as, for example, *To a Redbreast* and *To a Swallow* remind the reader strongly of John Clare (1793-1864) and his collection *Poems Descriptive of Rural Life* (1820). Davidson does not acknowledge Clare as an influence however (any more than the younger man Clare admits of an influence of Davidson upon *him*). Neither does Davidson mention his near contemporary Border poets Sir Walter Scott (1771-1832); John Leyden (1775-1811) or 'The Ettrick Shepherd' James Hogg (1770-1835) – whose son acted as publisher for *Leaves*. The works of near contemporary poets with strong connections specifically to the Morebattle district - James Thomson (1700-1748) author of *The Seasons* – a seminal work of first rank importance in European art and literature (not to mention Thompson's inspirational role in his nephew's design for Edinburgh's New Town and in helping precipitate

the French Revolution of 1789) - and Thomas Pringle (1789-1834) of Blakelaw, the great anti-slavery campaigner (and a fellow religious dissenter) – are likewise never referred to by Davidson.

8. It being the case that Davidson was born at Lempitlaw, the scene for his poem *The Witch's Cairn* is very likely to be *Witches' Cairn* on the adjacent farm of Kersquarter in Sprouston Parish (Ordnance Survey reference: NT774335). The recorded traditions of both Stichill and Mordington parishes (see the Old & New Statistical Accounts of Scotland for the relevant parishes) state that their *Witches Cairns* were the places where numerous unfortunates were burned alive in the great witch hunts which swept through the Scottish Borders in the seventeenth century. The original endnotes to this poem, incorporated at the back of the *Leaves* edition, tend very much to confirm this Kersquarter location: "the author informs the editor that this piece was suggested on seeing a stone near to where he tended cows in his youth, which tradition pointed out as the spot where those horrible tragedies of witch-burning were perpetrated". This lonely place on what was then the bleak and wind-swept Hadden Rig Common is now occupied by a dark and somewhat forbidding wood from whose little-visited northern edge magnificent views of Teviotdale, Tweeddale, Kelso and the Merse may nevertheless be obtained at sunset by those not in thrall to the superstitions of their ancestors. The surviving Sprouston Kirk Session Records for the 1640s do not record any of these actual witch burnings but (not that our poet appears to have known the involvement of his kinsman) they do record the name of the leading *warlock* in the village: *Dand Davidson.*

9. Information from the Davidson Family Genealogy compiled by Margret Davidson Kellam and Barbara Lucas of Latham, New York State, USA.

10. For the full inscription see *Roxburghshire Monumental Inscriptions: Hounam & Linton* (1995) p.16 no. 61. This records James Smith's age at death as 19 years. Fly Creek Cemetery, Otsego County (Lot 314) records his age at death as 49 years.

11. Jeffrey's judgement here has been the main spur to researching Davidson's life and to having his achievement appropriately commemorated. In the course of investigating his life, discovering the name of his wife (Christian Richardson) and the place of his death (Upper Chatto) has led only quite recently to identifying his family gravestone in Morebattle churchyard.(No. 163 in *Roxburghshire Monumental Inscriptions: Morebattle* (1997). The accompanying map on p.9 of this handbook shows clearly the exact location of Davidson's grave). The full inscription on Davidson's gravestone reads:

In memory of Christian Richardson spouse to Robert Davidson Morebattle who died 2.10.1843 aged 69 years also of their son John who died Nov. 1818 aged 14 months and of their daughter Isabel who died May 1819 aged 10 years also the above Robert Davidson who died at Upper Chatto 6. 4. 1855 aged 76 years.

So while Jeffrey was not correct in saying that Davidson had no memorial at all, he was correct in saying that Davidson had not been (and has not until now been) *commemorated as a poet* – a man who was "an honour to his class and to the district in which he lived".

Letter from Robert Davidson to his publisher John Hogg. The only example of Davidson's handwriting known to have survived.

Reproduced by kind permission of the National Library of Scotland MS2670 f.117.

AUTOBIOGRAPHY

OF

ROBERT DAVIDSON

DAY-LABOURER, MOREBATTLE

WRITTEN IN HIS SEVENTIETH YEAR

October, 1847.

I was descended from poor but honest parents, who, like
the great majority of mankind, had their bread to earn by
the sweat of their brows; so, of course, my patrimony was
poverty and toil, which, in agricultural districts, amount
to an unalterable entail. My education was in-
deed very limited, the schoolmaster having been but a
short way abroad. In those days there was much of the
valuable time of children wasted, and little progress made.
There are many now more advanced in learning at seven
or eight years of age than could, in former times, have
been found at twelve. In many country schools very
little attention was paid to spelling. Perhaps once a-week
we were made to spell the names of a few men, or the
names of some towns or villages; indeed, the only part of
my early education that I have never forgot is to mis-
spell.

There are great changes in the manners and modes
of life among the peasantry since my school-boy days.
The spinning-jenny had not then supplanted the spinning-
wheel, and the spinning-wheel had not altogether expelled

the distaff and rock. I remember several aged matrons, who, with that simple instrument of industry in their bosoms, used often to entertain groups of happy young-sters, gathered around their hearths in the winter even-ings, by telling them legendary tales of border barons and their bloody feuds; and they would sometimes croon over to us scraps of ancient ballads that had been the favourite songs of their youth; and although there was but little melody either in the air itself or in the voice of the songster, they were listened to with as much breathless attention as ever the strains of Madame Catalini or Jenny Lind could have been by the crowded audiences of a very different description. As superstition prevailed among the peasantry far more than it does now, we were often told fearful stories about fairies, brownies, and bogles, the truth of which the narrators themselves had not the least doubt of; and I can assure you we believed and trembled, for we always sat closer together, and drew nearer the fire. It has always been observed that early impressions are seldom altogether eradicated; and I have no doubt but that some who were then listeners, even when they had arrived at the years of manhood, when ex-posed to a dark night, may have sometimes looked around "with prudent cares".

When I was ten years of age I was hired to herd a few cows; as the country was then almost uninclosed, a good number of boys were wanted for the same employment. I had by that time a great inclination for reading, but there were few works in the possession of the peasantry at that time indeed. Very few cottages were without Boston's and Erskine's works – certainly an invaluable library; but their worth could not be properly appreciated by a boy of my age. I can never forget the extraordinary excitement and delight I felt when the history of Sir William Wallace fell first into my hands. What, I be-lieve, added much to the enjoyment was, that I thought it all as true as truth itself, and not the production of Blind Harry. I conclude, from my own experience, that no kind of reading, either for pleasure or profit, is equal to authentic history – truth being most congenial to the human mind; at least what we consider to be so. What makes children so fond of the tales of "Jack the Giant-Killer" and "Jack and the Bean-Stalk" is that they believe them to be true at that period of life. When "Barry's Collection" for schools came first into my hands it was a great treasure to me, there being nothing of the kind at the paltry school at which I was taught. When I read, in prose and verse, extracts from the works of the great writers that are inserted there, I felt as we may suppose Gulliver to have felt in his travels, when he was carried from a nation of pigmies among a race of giants; for up to this time I had seen little of the writing of profane authors but penny histories and ballads. I had attempted before this to compose some simple verses, of which, in my own mind, I was proud; but I found now that doggerel rhyme and poetry were two distinct things.

I continued to herd cattle in summer and to wait on them in winter until I went to learn to hold the plough. At that employment I continued six or seven years. In the twenty-first year of my age I was hired to a farmer who had a share in a country library, and who likewise got the newspapers once a-week; and as he cared little about reading himself, he was so good as to allow me to take out what books I had a mind to, and likewise to give me a reading of the papers duly. Until that time my acquaintance with books, or with what was passing in the world, was so limited that I never heard either of the name or of the works of Robert Burns, it being then two years after his death. I need scarcely say that I felt both astonishment and admiration of the poetry and powers of that extraordinary man.

My simple muse oft visited me at the plough and made

the labour to seem lighter and the day shorter. At that
time none of my fellow-servants knew anything as to how
I was employed, for I thought I would be laughed at. Gold-
smith says his poetry was his shame in crowds but his pride
in solitude; and I believe many a humble rhymster has
had the same feeling as that great poet. None of my at-
tempts at poetry were ever written down until I was married
and had a house of my own, where I had an opportunity
to write without any person knowing what was written.

I now took a house in Morebattle, and worked as a day-
labourer, and sometimes took jobs by the piece, which I
greatly preferred. At this employment a number of years
of heavy toil passed over my head, without ever giving me
a heavy heart. I had youth, and health, and a happy fire-
side; my children were then about me, and I was happy
in my partner in life, though her dowry was only truth,
honesty and prudence, and, I may add, a steady and con-
tented mind. I am convinced, both by observation and
experience, that a man's fireside is a source whence arises
his bitterest griefs or most exquisite pleasures. A man
is more than repaid for the toils of the day, if, at home,
there are eyes to mark his coming, and to look brighter
when he comes. I must say this was almost the happiest
part of my life. I was content with the station in which
Providence had placed me, - proud when I thought of the
country in which I lived, where the poorest peasant has
rights and dares assert them; but the road of life, like
the surface of the earth, has its ups and downs. In 1811,
wet seasons and late harvests raised the markets so much
that the wages of labour could not purchase provisions
equal to support life, to those who had large families, and
I had then a wife and six children. The situation I was
then placed in made me appear as an author, which, be-
fore, I had resolved not to do; for I knew that the public
allowed no mediocrity in poetry; therefore I could have
but little hope. Back seasons and dearths still continued,

so I was forced to betake myself to my old employment, the plough, as I got corn for my wages, which supplied my family with bread; and at this I continued until part of my family could do something for themselves. Then I again took a house in Morebattle, and wrought as a labourer; like the country mouse in the fable,

> "I sought again my hollow tree,
> My crust of bread, and liberty."

In 1824 I tried another publication of my little pieces, but, as respected profit, they did not do much. When I came to peruse the splendid poetry of the great men that were then living, I thought any attempt made by me to attract notice would be foolish as the glow-worm to light its feeble lamp in a twelve o'clock sun; and at two different times I destroyed all my papers, after they had accumulated to a good bulk, being convinced I was only troubling myself in vain; but my muse and I were like the honest webster and his wife – we could neither agree when together nor remain separate.

It is now fifty-three years that I have wrought a man's work; and in that period, like those who have travelled the way before me, I have seen both joys and sorrows. About four years since my wife died, and a short time after three sons went to America; and I am now taught that, as far as this world is concerned, all is vanity.

Thus I have given you an account of the different steps of my life, in which not much interest could be expected; indeed, excepting in the difference in years, it might be all contained in an epitaph written by Ben Jonson, which is –

> "Here lies who laugh'd and cried,
> Told five-and-fifty-years and died."

ROBERT DAVIDSON.

THE KIRN DAY

Nae mair the sprightly sangsters greet the morn,
  But pensive sit beneath the black'ning slae;
The haw hangs crimson'd on the leafless thorn;
  The nut-brown braken shades the distant brae:
While autumn forth his russet plenty shakes,
  Wide o'er the fertile fields profusion pours,
For brose and bannocks to the land of cakes,
  When, o'er her mountains, angry winter lours,
  Wi' a' his bitter-biting with'ring powers.

Before the distant sun had speel'd the height,
  And hail'd the woodlands with a cheerful smile,
Upon the furrow'd field, wi' hearts fu' light,
  A band of rustics plied their early toil:
Wi' sturdy hands they cow'd the noddin' grain,
  This day their rugged task they hope to end,
When they wad ca' their hard won fees their ain;
  With conscious joy their simple hearts distend,
As o'er the sheaf-clad glebe their forms they bend.

The auld guidman stalks round wi' mickle pride,
    And e'es the gowden grain in clustering raws;
Let ruthless Boreas wildly sweep the glade,
    He's heedless now o' every blast that blaws.
A constant crack gaes round among the fair,
    A' deeply versed in fashion's varying law;
Ilk ane recounts her stock, wi tentie care,
    O' breast-knots, top-knots, beads and bonnets braw,
    Or joins some envied beauty to misca'.

The gatherers hover round in straggling bands,
    To them a scanty portion autumn yields;
Contented still they pick, with feeble hands,
    The little remnants of the stubble fields:
Yet still they seem to share the common joy,
    That full this day in every face doth shine;
The aged matron tells the thoughtless boy,
    How many hairsts she'd seen and shorn langsyne,
    When she was brisk and braw in youthfu' prime.

Wi' serious air she tells o' unco' deeds
    Perform'd by warlocks in the lonely glen;
Converting broomsticks into stately steeds,
    To scour the wilds, unscared by marsh or fen;
Or what mishaps befell on festive nights,
    In days of yore, of which our minstrels sing;
How unperceiv'd approach'd the fairy knights,
    And stole the boasted beauties from the ring,
    Then fled to fairy-land on viewless wing.

Wi' themes like these, fu' fast the moments glide,
    Until the reekin' coggies reach the field;
Wi' right guid will the heuks are laid aside,
    And every hand a doughty horn doth wield:
In firm array they hem the bowies round;
    Cowr'd on the yird in circular ring they close;
Then rural tales and simple jests abound,
    When blithely clautin' at their cogs o' brose –
    Sae fared the hearts wha fought wi' great Montrose.

Perhaps some pamper'd spark, weak, wan, and pale,
    Whose gentle stomach ne'er was edged wi' toil,
May look disdainfu' on the simple meal,
    The wholesome produce of their native soil:
Though neither Ind has lent its baneful aid,
    To fill these humble cups with viands rare,
Yet on the cheek is rosy health pourtray'd
    Of hardy swains and rural beauties fair,
Fresh as the flow'rs which scent the morning air.

The call of nature stilled, loud clam'rous dins
    Among the sportive youngsters soon arise;
Among the elder core the crack begins,
    In full divan now met, lke statesmen wise;
Behind a stook fu' snugly they recline,
    The pipe and mill they freely hand about,
The kirk and state affairs they clear define,
    And solve each knotty point beyond a doubt,
    How dark intrigues and secret plots came out.

Anticipation paints the festive night –
   The moments quick on rapid pinions fly,
Till at the ca', with jovial hearts and light,
   They start, and keen their former toils they ply;
This wish'd for day, a wonted right they claim,
   Without restraint their boasted strength to try;
Wi' garrulous tongue begins a windy wight,
   To stir some quarrels that hae lang lain bye,
Then fierce defiance darts from every eye.

From right to left a furious fray begins,
   Each sober thought by madd'ning rage exiled;
Frae rig tae rig the bandster toddling rins,
   And a' is havoc and confusion wild:
The auld guidman, o' temper quite bereft,
   His bonnet shifts, and oft his haffet claws,
Tae see the hard won crop in handfu's left,
   A ready prey to cotters and to craws;
   He rins redwood, and shores them wi' the laws.

The softer sex, whose faces best beseem
   That witching smile which steals the heart away,
Now from their eyes shoot forth a fiercer beam,
   And kindle into ardour at the fray;
Till saftly soundin' yont the briery knowe,
   The distant note o' music strike their ears;
Then slow wi' bonnet blue and lyart pow,
   Their ancient minstrel, *Claw-the thairm* appears,
   And is received wi' loud and jovial cheers.

Though gentles may his uncouth touch deride,
    They roose him here, and say he's deeply skill'd;
Into a calm their frenzies soon subside –
    Discord on sooty pinions leaves the field,
Scared by the magic of those matchless airs
    That Caledonia proudly ca's her ain;
Which oft have soothed the lover's bleeding cares,
    And cheer'd her warriors on the bloody plain,
When pressing forward o'er red heaps of slain.

The auld guidman forgets his anger now,
    Again guid humour twinkles in his e'e;
Frae rig to rig he blithely staggers through,
    And tells his auld warld tales wi' mirth and glee;
He bids a youngster take the auld grey mare,
    And speed him swiftly to the market town,
To bring a cordial brisk, their hearts to cheer,
    A cog of nappy ale, both stout and brown,
To banish care, and synde their sorrows down,

When their rough task near a conclusion draws,
    Thick, struggling round it, keen the lasses burn;
They think to whom the hin'most handfu' fa's,
    Shall meet wi' Hymen ere the Hairst return:
Urged wi' despair, a maid bangs fiercely on,
    Some towmonds syne she'd life's meridian speel'd;
A rival hacks her finger to the bone,
    She in a passion, ragin' leaves the strife,
While, at her hap, loud laugh and jibes are rife.

Now, high in air, they caps and bonnets fling;
　　The shouts of joy from ev'ry tongue resound;
The glens and valleys long responsive ring;
　　The distant mountains back return the sound:
Thrice happy vales! Nought breaks your silence still,
　　Except the reaper's shout or milkmaid's sang;
In days of yore, oft did the bugle shrill,
　　Wake all your echoes with its rousing clang,
　　When steel-clad warriors sternly rush'd alang.

Then lawless bands, by glen or wizard stream,
　　Like ruthless tigers prowling for their prey,
Did wait the rising of the lunar beam,
　　To sweep the fenceless flocks and herds away.
As rural toil his rugged labour plies,
　　He fears not now to lose his due reward,
While law stands sentinel with eagle eyes,
　　A firm, unshaken, and undaunted guard,
　　And awes wild rapine with his shining sword.

Yet on the fields where law and freedom reign,
　　A demon stalks, with outward splendour graced,
Converting the once crowded, cheerful plain,
　　Into a dreary, desolated waste!
See ruin'd hamlets in his track appear!
　　In distant lands their former inmates mourn;
If powerful fate check not his wild career,
　　His breath will blast the palace in her turn,
　　And lay fair freedom in her awful urn.

FASTEN E'EN

Where Beaumont laves with limpid waves,
  That bright reflect the day;
Or dimpling deep, with eddying sweep,
  Down fertile valleys stray,
A jovial core, with social roar,
  Was form'd in phalanx deep,
In sport and play, to pass the day,
  Their Fasten E'en to keep,
      Fu' blithe that day.

The ploughs stand idle down the dale,
  Fast frae the fell the shepherd hies,
The barnman drops his weary flail,
  No more his task the ditcher plies;
The dusty miller sets his mill,
  The souter cast his apron,
Through a' the town the looms stand still,
  The wabster's lads are vap'rin
      Fu' crouse that day.

The schoolboy trips wi' brisker pace,
    His heart loups light and cheerie;
Pleasure's blinkin' in his face,
    Nae tasks to make him eerie;
Even hirplin' age new vigour gains,
    And seems mair brisk and sprightly;
He casts his laid o' cramps and pains,
    And on his crutch leans lightly
        On sic a day.

Then slily through the circle deep,
    That round the cocks are closin'
Wi' anxious e'e the youngsters peep;
    The victor-bird supposin';
No leaders more suspense could know,
    Where kingdoms' fate depended,
When front to front, at Waterloo,
    Renowned hosts contended,
        That unco day.

The ruthless rivals foot the ring,
    And a' their plumage staining,
In deadly dint wi' beak and wing,
    The life drops freely draining;
Though hearts are barb'rous and profane
    That smile on life expiring,
A virtue lurks beneath the stain,
    When valour they're admiring
        On sic a day.

When high in air the ba' was flung,
   Fu' lightly off they bounded,
Then lang and loud the clamour rung,
   Till a' the hills resounded;
Whiles sweeping wildly cross the vale,
   Whiles o'er the uplands bending,
Whiles struggling stoutly down the dale,
   Like meeting streams contending,
        Fu' keen that day.

We see that ardent spirit blaze,
   Which o'er these hills presided,
When deadly feuds of former days,
   Made sterner fields decided;
But now we share that quiet sweet,
   Which gentle peace imposes,
Save when on Fasten E'en we meet,
   Wi' broken shins or noses,
        On sic a day.

Sin' first the glintin' morning sun,
   Was o'er the hills appearing,
Wi' drouthy comrades, *Burniewin'*
   Had kept the stoup a-steering;
When he had scared the cares away,
   That dogg'd him for a towmont,
And staggerin' out to join the fray,
   Fell o'er the lugs in Beaumont,
        Fu' deep that day.

The souter's wife hang by his hair,
  And sair misca'd her deary' –
This day he'd spent a crown and mair,
  Her very tongue was weary;
He lap, and freed him frae her paw',
  But still retained the scar o't,
He frisk'd away to chase the ba';
  And glad she made nae mair o't'
      On sic a day.

When gloamin' keek't out o'er the hill,
  They wish'd then to retard her;
The contest then grew sterner still,
  With keen redoubled ardour;
The ploughman laddies plied their heels,
  To gain the gree they ettle,
The manly limb that Cheviot speels,
  Exerted a' his mettle
      On sic a day.

Tam Coplin lang had viewed the play,
  And laugh'd to see them toiling,
But still he scorned to join the fray,
  His breeks ower braw for soiling:
But oh, what reck! A moorlan' chiel
  Came friskin by like fire,
Wi' wicked tae tipped Tammie's heel,
  And turned him in the mire,
      Right o'er that day.

When night's dull dusky wing at last,
  Had hill and valley shrouded,
Into the town they gather fast,
  Ilk change-house nook is crowded;
Though doubtless now the game is changed,
  Yet still they're stoutly striving,
In raws on forms and benches ranged,
  And at the dumplings driving
      Fu' fast that night.

When fiddler Will had screwed his pins,
  And tried *her* temper tightly,
Each wight forgot his broken shins,
  And lap both lang and lightly;
Now rural beauties try their power,
  And round the ring are shining,
How best to grace the social hour,
  Are a' their arts combining
    On sic a night.

Here sit some chaps that hae nae taste,
  For music or for lasses,
Snugly around a bunker placed,
  Weel clad wi' jugs and glasses;
Their loud huzzas, and frantic shouts,
  And clam'rous bursts of laughter,
Soon drown'd the fiddler's feeble notes,
  And shook both roof and rafter
      Wi' din that night.

Then but and ben the landlord flew,
   And wow, but he was happy,
And still the tither mutchkin drew,
   Or stoups o' reamin nappy;
Till stretch'd beside the toddy stout,
   Low lay poor Dick the souter:
The miller bore Sir *Haprick* out
   Just like a bag o' mu'ture,
      Sae drunk that night!

SEQUEL TO FASTEN E'EN

Just was this picture once in days of yore-
Now rural sports and pastimes are no more;
Fled, ah, for ever fled on wayward wing,
Save in these lowly vales of which I sing.
Here, independence lingers, loath to part,
Diffusing gladness o'er the peasant's heart –
In vain your loit'ring, dear celestial maid,
On your loved haunts, now field to field is laid;
The tinsell'd trash of gaudy grandeur waves,
And haughty lordlings frown on servile slaves.
Who would not wish our fathers' happier lot,
When every shed could claim its little spot!
Although no dainties crown'd the simple board,
But what their native mountains did afford!
Poor but contented at the healthsome plough,
They, from the spot they till'd subsistence drew;
Warm in their breast their love of country burn'd,
They had an interest in the soil they turn'd!

Hail independence! Nurse of every art
Which brightens life, or elevates the heart!
Beneath thy ray the virtues raise their head,
Fair fertile source of every gen'rous deed;
Thy smile more noble makes the simple swain,
Than all the fops in grandeur's gilded train; –
Thy pupil Donald, on his mountain free,
With two attendants, poverty and thee;
Or when he's sever'd from his hills afar,
And marshall'd in the flaming front of war,
Even there, he doth thy inbred fire display,
Which blazes bright on danger's darkest day.
Where'er thy cheering influence is found,
There, rural mirth and manly sports abound;
But when unwieldy wealth, with baneful sway,
Doth sweep the peasants from their cots away,
In gloomy silence, o'er once cheerful plains,
A dead'ning death-like melancholy reigns.

SIM AND SANDY

Sim and Sandy, as our shepherds tell,
Were old companions on the bentie fell;
They lived in friendship from their earliest day,
Till restless time had turn'd their haffets grey:
Nae langer fit to speel the mountain's side,
And guard the hirsels in their wand'rings wide,
By weakness forced to try an easier turn,
And tend the hawkies down the braken burn.
Twice forty times they'd seen the vernal gale
Wave the lone wild-flowers on the banks of Kail;
As oft they'd seen the brown leaf quiv'ring fa',
And stately Cheviot row'd in sheets o' snaw;
The friends they had in former days were gane,
And left them wand'ring life's rough road their lane!
Dull wintry age few buds o' friendship yields,
They'd now grown strangers on their native fields:
To them the simmer sun had ceased to warm,
And smiling nature tint her power to charm;

Sick of the world that once to their young eyes
Appear'd a flow'ring paradise of joy –
Some shapeless heaps, with hemlocks wild between,
Still mark'd the spot where cottages had been;
But now no longer the abodes of men –
Lone silence slumbered in the lovely glen.
Near by the ruins row'd a crystal burn,
And half enclosed them with a circling turn;
Its waters shaded from the scorching beam,
With weeping willows bending o'er the stream;
Some aged trees, with fading branches bare,
Shed o'er the scene a melancholy air.
Here oft they met to soothe each other's waes,
And tell the tales of long elapsed days;
Upon the spot where their first breath they drew,
And where the happy days of childhood flew.
One day they met upon their favourite spot,
And traced the ruins of each well-known cot;
Propt on their staffs, they totter'd, weak and wan,
Then made a stand, when Sandy thus began:

SANDY

Ah! waes my heart! What desolation's here:
Yet still to us these ruin'd heaps are dear;
Our first impressions leave a lasting trace,
That a' the storms of life can ne'er deface.
Foul fa' the ruthless hand that has erased
The hearths on which the cheerful ingles blazed;

Where oft we join'd the happy circles bright,
That ring'd them round to pass the winter's night.
When guileless sports no longer could engage,
We sat attentive to the tales of age:
How parted worth tyrannic pride defied,
How warriors struggled, and how martyrs died!
Yon aged hawthorn (once with blossoms gay),
Which mocks the spring, and hastens to decay,
Reminds us where, on simmer gloamings sweet,
The cheerful village train were wont to meet;
No children now in joyful bands are seen,
To pu' the wild flowers on the fairy green;
No more they give their scents to human kind,
But shed their odours on the senseless wind.

SIM

The very thought is like to blind my e'e,
To think what changes we have lived to see –
A croft converted to a sheep walk wild,
Where twenty separate happy harvests smiled;
Their owners, free from servitude and strife,
Found peace and plenty through the blink of life!
But now these pleasing scenes have disappear'd,
Around their former haunts no sounds are heard,
Save when the bittern wheels wi' dreary moans,
Or lonely lapwing screams in plaintive tones –
Such is the devastation splendour makes,
And mis'ry waits on every step she takes;

The peasant's forced from his native shed,
The much-loved walks where his forefathers stray'd —
In endless wand'rings round he's restless toss'd,
Till in his breast the love of country's lost;
He flies for shelter to distant climes,
Or crowded towns, to swell the tide of crimes.

SANDY

What ye have said ower plainly doth appear,
Our braw new laird has made a desert here:
Wi' Indian gowd he bought the birken cleugh,
Howe'er it came, it's there, and that's aneugh —
These gowden countries maun be hapless parts;
They're rowth o' gear, but scant o' gallant hearts
To combat on their injured country's side,
And form a bulwark 'gainst opposition's side,
Upon their shores each hungry harpy flocks,
Aneugh to fleece them to the naked rocks;
By hook or crook his empty pouches fills,
Returns to Scotland and buys half her hills —
The fact is plain in our vain birkie's case,
His canty sire was fiddler to his grace;
But now the son can with his patron vie,
Nae duke or marquis wears his cap sae high;
Mair senseless pride I've seen his gowkship shaw,
Than Scotland's nobles hae amang them a'.
Ae day he hunted in the braken slack,
Twa foreign flunkies cringing at his back;

I chanced to meet him as I turn'd the kye,
And let sir Foplin strut unheeded by –
Likewise my luckless collie did neglect
To pay to gentle dogs a due respect;
A surly hound salutes him wi' a snack,
He seized it firm and turned it on its back;
His honour storm'd, and aim'd a deadly shot –
Which laid my collie sprawling on the spot –
Some twa three breathings past ere I could speak,
My wee drap bluid ran burning to my check:
As I drew near him – off his gelding sprung,
Or, by the powers aboon, he'd felt my rung.

SIM

Lang sair'd by servile slaves ayont the seas,
Wi' restless bonnets and wi' souple knees –
Where heartless man, debased, degraded, quakes –
At his return he bans the land o' cakes,
Whose hardy sons, by slav'ry yet unbroke,
Have sauls as stubborn as their native oak,
Untutored how to cringe, or prostrate fa',
To naught submissive but their country's law;
The manly airs that on their brows preside,
Seem rustic rudeness viewed by empty pride;
Yet they're the fairest flowers our country yields,
And firmest props on hard contested fields.

They might hae clatter'd nonsense lang aneugh,
Had not a cry resounded down the cleugh;
Sent by a shepherd on a distant brae,
To warn them that their kye were gaun astray.

THE WITCH'S CAIRN

A TALE

Is there no old shepherd a story can tell
About that old cairn on the edge of the fell?
Midst all my researches, I never can know
Who reared the pile, or who slumbers below;
Perhaps some brave hero, whose daring and might
Has turn'd for his country the balance of fight;
Perhaps some proud chieftain, whose fate we'll ne'er learn,
Who soared at a kingdom and found but a cairn!
Not so said a shepherd, this cairn keeps a name
That better had dwelt with oblivion than fame;
Not hero nor chieftain, in story be praised,
To Meg of the cavern this bourick was raised –
Come, sit ye down by me below this green tree,
And I'll tell ye the tale as old shepherds told me:
When done, ye shall see in yon lone glen sae grey,
The stream where she drank, and the cave where she lay.

This witch, for some time, kept the country aghast,
But vengeance o'erhied her and crush'd her at last –

Twas when her black cantrips no more could be borne,
The country assembled by hundreds one morn;
Then some of the boldest seized Meg in her cell,
Before she had leisure to practice her spell.
Her hands they with saplings of rowin tree bound,
They bore her in triumph and shouted around;
The judge being seated upon a grey stone,
The crowd ranged around him, the trial went on;
Some kept at a distance, and durst not come near –
Tho' Meg was in fetters, they e'ed her with fear.

Auld Bauldy the blacksmith, first Maggie accused –
Says he, by her pranks, I've been sadly abused;
I met her at morn ere the sun came in view,
That luckless encounter I ever may rue;
The glance that she shot me from her dark drumlie e'e,
Forever has kipel'd misfortune and me:
Nine times ere the e'enin' my knuckles I brunt,
My bellows broke down, and the lum gaed alunt;
I went to the fowling and shot my ain drake;
Next morning, poor crummy was cauld at the stake;
I gaed the last week tae a tryst on the Tweed,
But her cursed cantrips bewildered my head –
I missed the ford in the broad light of day,
And ne'er fand the bottom 'tween bank or 'tween brae;
When dreepin' and chitterin' I took the road hame,
My beast fell aneath me as dead as a stane –
Tae flee frae misfortune 'tis needless to strive,
We ne'er can be sinder'd while Maggie's alive.

Then Sandy, the shepherd, began a sad tale,
His eye turn'd on Maggie: he paused and grew pale;
Says he, I've done nothing deserving her spite,
Although she's attempted to ruin me quite:
She passed me one day as I tented my flock,
My unmannered collie but tugged at her cloak;
But poor luckless Yarrow I never saw mair,
He ran to the mountains as wild as a hare.
Before I cam' hame, she had witch'd my best cow,
I seized the hag, and drew blood on her brow;
I thought by my daring to baffle the spell,
But soon her dread vengeance was felt on the fell!
The sun had gaed down, and the ev'ning was still,
The flocks on the moorlands were wand'ring at will,
No token of tempest was seen in the skies,
And nothing but magic could make one arise –
Soon, broken and dull grew the sound of the rills,
And deep hollow murmurs were heard on the hills,
A thick murky gloom soon extinguish'd the day,
And night seemed impatient to witness the fray;
So wild was the tempest that burst on the heath,
That all things that breathed were threatened with death,
The moorcock was choked ere a covert he found,
The strong winged raven was dash'd to the ground,
The loud rolling thunder groan'd through the dark drift,
The red winged bolt shook the mountain's grey clift,
The rocks, rent to splinters, their beds did forgo,
And roll'd with a crash to the valleys below!

Bent to the yird by the hurricane's shock,
I crawl'd on all fours to a cave in the rock,
There trembled in terror till midnight was past,
Expecting each moment would count for my last;
Then in the dark cavern, I heard a deep grane –
A hand touched my haffet, as cauld as a stane!
My hair heaved my bonnet – my breathing grew low –
My staff shook like aspen, and dropt on the snow –
I sprang from the cavern as swift as the wind,
And ne'er cast a look to the mountains behind!
When brambles and brushwood entangled my shins,
I snapt them like threads that the gossamer spins.
My auld aunt Bess gat a horrible fright,
She's never done weel since that terrible night;
She swears that she saw the auld beldam ride past,
Astride on a broomstick, directing the blast –
Full many a storm I have faced in my day,
But reckon'd with this, they seem'd breezes in May.

Next morning the fragments of hirsels were found;
In wreath-choked torrents some hundreds were drown'd –
Some, by the rude tempest, dash'd o'er the wide fens,
And some, undiscovered, lie yet in the glens.
No doubt but the court will judge candid and fair,
But if they spare Maggie, I'll never herd mair.

Then Watty, the wabster, ran wild through the crowd,
His plaint against Maggie was bitter and loud –

Gae burn her, says Watty, and end her ill life,
That vile imp of Satan's bewitched my wife:
Weel a' our guid neighbours can freely attest,
That o' the guid housewives, my Elspeth's was best;
Sae cleanly, sae thrifty, in but or in ben,
Until this auld witch came to win in the glen –
Dung diled wi' her cantrips, she sauntered away,
And followed the troopers for many a day;
Now when she's returned, she'll do nought for the loom,
She's never at rest when the ale caps are toom;
She makes the house echo wi' clamour and war,
She drinks like a souter, and swears like a tar;
I've spent my last farthing to pay of her scores,
Now naked starvation has enter'd my doors,
Nor comfort, nor kindness, my sorrow relieves,
For Elspeth repays me wi' naught but her neeves.
Yestreen, frae the alehouse, I brought her hame fou',
The bumps o' the pint stoup remain on my brow;
This hag is the cause of my sorrow and shame,
The person bewitched is naethin to blame;
I hope that your honours will grant my request,
I've brought twa tar barrels, we'll kindle the best.

The judge who presided was held in renown,
He once was a chaplain, and served the crown;
He fought at red Flodden, and never stained steel,
But came off unrivalled for swiftness of heel;
Proud learning her treasures had shower'd on his head;
He travell'd, when young, 'twixt the Tyne and the Tweed;

The wide fields of science he clearly could scan,
His study was woman – I dare not say man;
His fame as a judge flew o'er land and o'er sea,
For none came before him that ever got free.
Upon the rude rabble he turned his eyes,
Said little, or nothing, for wisdom's concise –
Half-bent with a burden of judgement and sense,
He called upon Maggie to make her defence.

Says Maggie in magic I never was skill'd,
I think it a weapon no mortal can wield.
Can mortals make tempests arise and be still,
Or agitate nature and soothe her at will?
Will mind and dull matter serve 'neath their employ,
Or sunshine and shadow, or sorrow and joy?
Were fate for a moment the task to resign,
It fits not an arm that is feeble like mine.
Some say, I'm deputed by demons to vent
Their malice on mortals that ne'er can be spent;
To mar each fair prospect, and tempt them to sin,
And blast the few joys that are scatter'd so thin.
If demons have such a dread gift in their power,
I would not receive it for worlds told o'er,
I feel for each heart that's with sorrow opprest,
Could wishing relieve them, they soon should be blest;
For this was a lesson I learned from woe –
To value a friend and to pity a foe;
For long ere my day had begun to decline,
Pale grief was a guest in this bosom of mine;

War, cruel war, was the cause of my pain,
My heart's dearest partner in battle was slain;
He went with a foray no more to return,
And left me bewilder'd in sorrow to mourn –
He left me a mother to valour and worth,
From me, six brave yeomen derived their birth.
When stately, and blooming in life's lovely spring,
They all fell on Flodden, abreast with their king;
I hasted away to bedew their sad biers,
With tears of a mother – the saltest of tears.
The victors exulting, had buried the brave,
Unshrouded, they slept in one wide bloody grave!
To life's fleeting pleasures I then bade adieu,
The banks of the Yarrow grew irksome to view;
No more they seemed lovely, delightful and gay,
The flowers that adorn'd them were faded for aye;
All wretched and helpless, bereaved of those
Who soothed life's sorrows, and shelter'd its close,
Some forced, by hunger, a morsel to crave,
I made my abode in that dark dreary cave.
When pity denies me, I wander forlorn,
And pick the cold berry that's left on the thorn:
My couch in the cavern is flinty and hard –
If demons employ me, how poor's my reward!
If I am condemned, few days I can lose,
My latest are closing, beclouded with woes!
Of death's darksome stream I have reached the brim,
My life's like a lamp that is dying and dim.

I'm lonely and friendless – the last of my race –
None share in my sorrows, or fear my disgrace –
The hearts that once lov'd me, are sunk in that sleep,
Where spirits may pity, but eyes cannot weep.

When two rushing torrents do thwart in their course,
They're both for a moment bereft of their force!
Swift o'er the wide crowd rose a short broken sigh,
And a mild beam of pity shone in each eye.

A friar came forward and spoke in the ring,
Then reason and pity fled both on swift wing:
The fiends, says the friar, have formed a plan,
That has for its object the mis'ry of man;
The brownie, the kelpy, the wizard and fae,
All serve in their legions, and share in their pay;
The tricks and manoeuvres they learn from their chief,
If not well attested might stagger belief –
A witch, when she chooses, all shapes can assume,
A hare on the hill, or a tod in the broom;
'Tween midnight and morning to Lapland she'll roam,
And skim the wide ocean as light as the foam,
Or cleave the thin air, when to flight she's inclined,
She'll mount on a moonbeam, and distance the wind;
Sometimes, for her pastime, she tempests the floods,
And makes the blue billows to lash the dark clouds,
Then laughs as proud navies, distress'd in the strife,
Hung high on the surges, and struggling for life –

Nine times to the wainward she's waved a black wand,
Then pale sheeted spectres rise at her command,
They frolic, they gambol, they join in the dance,
With carles from England, and carlins from France:
She lilts to their steps with an eriesome croon,
That startles dull midnight and darkens the moon –
Though Meg has been canting 'bout poortith and grief,
A witch I can prove her, and one of the chief –
The charges against her are weighty and clear,
We ne'er saw such blunders till Maggie came here;
Impelled by her patron, her skill she put forth,
To blast the appearance of virtue and worth.
A monk in our convent, you once loved so dear –
This hag has disgraced him – oh pardon his tear!
She called up a fiend in his likeness array'd,
And show'd him in sunshine concern'd with a maid –
No mortal's more free of maid, widow or wife,
No snow on the Cheviot's more pure than his life;
For on that same day, I can freely declare,
He was in the convent, engaged in prayer;
But ah, this vile hag's laid his fame in the lurch,
A vile trick of Satan to scandal the church.

Poor Maggie was roasted, the country found rest,
But harden'd in witchcraft, she never confess'd –
Around yon old cairn, where her ashes were spread,
No verdure is foster'd, nor dew-drops are shed;
All seems to be deaf to the voice of the spring,
Within the rank hemlocks that skirt the dark ring.

At eve, when the maukin steals through the tall fern,
Amidst her wild wandering, she shuns this dread cairn;
Or when the dull screech-owl glides o'er the scorched stones,
It quickens her motion and deepens her tones:
At morn, when the lark with his loftiest lay,
Awakens the sangsters and welcomes the day,
When from the grey cloud he beholds the dread spot,
He darts to a distance, and alters his note –
Here, fame says, grim spectres have often appear'd,
And voices not mortal by shepherds have heard;
Both reason and instinct the cemet'ry shun –
Thus proving 'tis haunted as clear as the sun.

THE CHEVIOT GAMES

Frae south'ran climes the spring returns,
   Wi' joy creation e'es him;
Frae frozen fetters start the burns,
   And wander on in freedom.
Again the lav'rock strains his throat,
   That's lang been sealed in sadness,
The lintie lilts his blythsome note,
   The grove resounds wi' gladness
         An' joy this day.

Fast to a spot 'mang Cheviot knowes,
   Come herds an' collies thrangin,
Where arrows keen, frae border bows,
   On former days were twangin;
But now on happier errants meet,
   To hand the games o' Cheviot,
And keep the pint stoup reekin' het,
   Lads baith frae Tyne and Tiviot
         Are here this day.

A band o' bang and sturdy chiels,
   A' buskit in their plaidies,
Bred up on Scotia's heathery hills,
   The wale o' a' her laddies,
Auld cronies kindly questions spier
   Whene'er they do forgather;
How collie rins, how thrive the gear,
   An' how they stood the weather
         Yon drifty day.

The thick'ning crowd swarms on the bent,
  Each face looks blithe and frisky,
While Tam is rearing up the tent,
  To hap the wee drap whisky;
Ilk breast beats light in jovial tift,
  Joy reigns, nought dare molest her,
Auld canker'd care is turn'd adrift,
  That us'd to plague and pester
        On other days.

Out owre the moor they chace the ba',
  Baith far and high they heave it;
Now souple limbs their mettle shaw,
  Bred on the braes o' Cheviot.
But frae this sport they soon withdraw,
  They quickly cease their skipping,
Unto a ring they gather a',
  To see the birkies stripping
        To race this day.

Away they start wi' nimble feet,
  The paltry prize despising,
For fame, for fame, their bosoms beat –
  It's honour that their prizing;
This phantom's lang been in request,
  Tho' chas'd in different fashion,
The peasant's an' the monarch's breast,
  Baith own the kindred passion
        On ony day.

Back owre the moor they bend their way,
   Wi' rapid stride they scrieve it,
Baith clean an' clear the wind-pipes play,
   That drink the streams o' Cheviot.
Now near the goal they furious push,
   Like mountain roes they're bounding,
The scatter'd crowds together rush,
   Their praises loud resounding
       That win this day.

The game is chang'd wi' pithy spald,
   The pand'rums stane they're swingin',
And then some sirrahs, young and yald,
   To gain the prize are springin'.
On other press'd, the clust'ring crowd
   Can scarcely keep frae quarrels,
While victor chiels strut aff as proud,
   As Caesar crown'd wi' laurels
       In days of yore.

Forfauchin sair, wi' various pranks,
   Unto a ring they gather,
Then hurkle down to ease their shanks,
   Soft seated on the heather.
At length the wrestlers appear,
   As bang an' sturdy fellows
As ever bore a border spear,
   Or scour'd the field wi' Wallace
       On ony day.

They grapple firm wi' pithy paws,
 An', when the prize is gained,
Maist part o' them's won nought but fa's,
 When every nerve's been strained.
Now to the tent they thrang an' squeeze,
 For a' the games are endit,
To gie their hearts a wee bit heeze,
 They fast the bicker bendit
  Wi' birr that day.

At ithers' heels the healths flew round,
 Their movements quick and quicker,
Till every cank'ring care was drown'd
 Amang the draps o' liquor.
There sat some chaps, no new begun,
 Right keen o' picking quarrels,
Wha came some miles to see the fun,
 But saw nought but the barrels
  An' stoups that day.

Frae words to blows at length they gang,
 Baith sticks an' nerves are skelpin',
(Some collies crushed amang the thrang,
 Wi' fearfu' din are yelpin').
They stagger'd hame in unco guise,
 Owre ilka stane they stumbled;
Sure whisky best deserves the prize,
 For he has monyest tumbled
  Right o'er this day.

While feebler chiels divert themsels,
　　To masquerades resorting,
Lang may the lads of Scotia's fells
　　Keep up their manly sporting!
It steel'd the hearts, it nerv'd the arms,
　　Of Greeks, when in their glory,
When often laid the Persian swarms
　　On bluidie beds an' gorie
　　　　　On former days.

THE TERM DAY

Auld nature wore her gayest garb o' green,
　　The fields look'd fresh an' gay wi' kindly show'rs,
The landscape thro' the mist was dimly seen,
　　The draps hung glitterin' on the bells o' flow'rs;
The eastern sky seem'd deeply ting'd wi' red,
　　At length Sol's flaming coursers upward spring,
His rays beam faintly on the mountain's head,
　　And sklentin' mildly, gild the lav'rock's wings,
As pois'd in air his morning notes he sings.

The hinds an' cottars now had left their beds,
　　Already a' the country's in a steer,
The day is come that they main shift their sheds,
　　Again the hand o' time's row'd round the year.
The drowsy weans, torn frae their repose,
　　Amid the uproar, wond'ring lift their e'en;
Blessed wi' the peace that innocence bestows,
　　They little care whate'er the stir may mean,
As yet but strangers to life's bust'ling scene.

The thriftie housewife packs her brittle ware,
　　The stools and forms are a' turn'd out o' doors,
They in an instant make the cottage bare,
　　And rob poor baudrons o' her favourite bores.
To clade the weans they toil'd, they tugg'd an' wrought,
　　The guidwife gies her dustie board a clean,
Then ben the house the drivers a' are brought,
　　And placed around to try her hamely cheer,
"Make free", she says, "this comes but ance a year".

A gleam of gladness sparkles in their eyes,
   A day is come that they can ca' they own,
Before a day like this to them arise,
   A tedious year must o'er their heads be flown.
O freedom! charmer of the human heart,
   That breast is cold that doth not feel thy pow'r;
Tho' oft the poor are forc'd with thee to part,
   Thy visit's sweet, tho' only for an hour,
Tio them who're forced 'neath lordly pride to cow'r.

Now a' in motion is the lowly band,
   The loaded teams move slowly out the way,
Some o' the weans, led in their mother's hand,
   Halt on the spots where they'd been used to play.
In little time they're wearing out o' sight,
   The weel-kenn'd haunts begin to disappear,
The tentie sire looks aft if a' be richt;
   While hawkie, routin', fetches up the rear,
She's a' their stock o' either goods or gear.

On ilka hand the length'ning rows appear,
   Of horses, carts, an' kye a blended thrang,
Their mixed din breaks hearsely on the ear,
   Owre moor an' dale the noisy clamour rang.
Athwart the country different airts they steer,
   Yet a' their shifting's seldom for the best,
Strong hope still bears them up frae year to year,
   An' cheers their hearts when sair wi' hardships press'd,
Tho' oft she cheats them, still she is caress'd.

What odds o' trav'llers on the road o' life,
   Some clogg'd wi' fetters, others wear a crown,
Some wade their weary way 'mang toil an' strife,
   While some are borne sae saft on beds o' down.
O never view them wi' your proud disdain,
   Ye sons o' affluence, sae fully fed,
Let pity's eye look softly on their pain,
   Who're doom'd to labour for their scanty bread,
An' for a wee bit shed to hide their head.

Spurn back mean flattr'y, list to truth at length,
   They're to their country no less dear than you,
They are the nerves that constitute her strength,
   Ye're but the feathers waving on her brow.
An' if that hapless day should ever dawn,
   That shows a hostile army on her shore,
She'll look to them to take her by the hand,
   And pay her ransom wi' a tide o' gore
On death's red field, where thund'ring cannons roar.

How sad these lands where mankind cannot make
   A change of masters, and a change of toil!
But, by a despot's chain, as to a stake,
   The hapless peasant's tether'd to the soil.
They have a tyrant's haughty frown to fear,
   While in their grief-torn breasts joy finds no room,
They see the end of each revolving year,
   Without one ray of hope to fill the gloom;
In vain to them doth nature richly bloom.

THE POOR MAN'S FUNERAL

The muse has often rifled fancy's fields,
  To wreathe a laurel for ambition's brow,
Forgot the virtues that the cottage yields,
  Or scorn'd the humble spot on where they grow.

Yet, from this source the wealth of nations flows,
  Upon this base the lofty palace stands;
'Tis they alone, when hostile tempest blows,
  That form the bulwark of their native lands.

A lowly peasant, in his lonely cot,
  Endured life's various ills with heart resign'd,
Without repining at his humble lot,
  Convinced he'd got the share of heaven design'd.

And, when he found his race was nearly run,
  Life's weary day fast drawing to a close,
With calm content he view'd its setting sun,
  For on his soul a brighter prospect rose.

His weeping children crowded round his bed,
  And forward press'd to take their last adieu,
In sorrow drown'd, no feigned tears were shed,
  With bleeding hearts his features pale to view.

He strove himself their drooping hearts to cheer,
  A lustre bright religion lends to woe,
Altho' their parting did demand a tear,
  They hop'd to meet where tears no more could flow.

He charg'd them, in whate'er they did engage,
   Their inner end to keep before their eye,
Amidst the pursuits of this bustling stage,
   They've nothing learn'd, who have not learn'd to die.

He then besought, with reverence profound,
   The God of grace, where all his hopes reposed –
That he would guide them thro' life's devious round,
   And to himself receive them when it closed.

He could no more; for nature's ebbing stream
   Within their channels would no longer roll,
Yet in his e'e was hope's triumphant beam,
   Till, from her feeble prison burst the soul.

Let sceptics own religion's power divine,
   And mark the grandeur of a Christian faith,
It makes celestial hopes bright beaming shine
   Through clouds that hover o'er the vale of death.

It paints an Eden in immortal bloom,
   Which no disease, nor misery invades;
Dispels annihilation's horrid gloom,
   That's scarce inferior to infernal shades.

How far superior is this honest worth,
   To that false greatness that the world admires,
Which on its species pours destruction forth,
   And, red with slaughter, on the field expires!

We seldom try the justice of their cause,
   Nor weigh the motives that their flags unfurl,
Whether to break oppressions iron jaws,
   Or chase the form of freedom from the worl'.

Wi' friends convened, and neighbours gather'd round,
  To the churchyard they slowly bend their way,
Now to commit, with decency profound,
  The lifeless body to its kindred clay.

No gaudy trappings deck the humble bier,
  No hacknied mourners mock the solemn scene;
His mournful children shed the genuine tear,
  From nature's native feelings strong an' keen.

As o'er his narrow house they look'd their last,
  They deem'd not tears a weakness, nor a crime,
While restless mem'ry sought the joys long past,
  And dragg'd their shadows up the stream of time.

The earliest friend they found on life's rough coast,
  Is to the grave's devouring jaws a prey;
Deep in the heart the tie is wove an' crost –
  The tendrest fibres bleed when torn away.

With gen'rous hearts they feel each other's woe,
  While natural kindness animates the whole,
And round their parent's tomb, the friendly glow
  Doth rouse the finest feelings of the soul.

But, round these base entailments envy clings,
  And disappointment rankles in the breast,
It shocks affection in its purest springs
  To see in one the plunderer of the rest.

His flatt'ry fawns the sons of power upon
  And scarce forsakes them with the fleeting breath,
She makes her last faint efforts on their tomb,
  When they have enter'd the domains of death.

Yet oft their names, like inundations vast,
  Are held in memory for destruction done:
While gentler streams do glide unnoticed past,
  And to the ocean of oblivion run.

THE GRAVE O' BRUCE

There's nane deserves the name o' Scot,
 Whose bosom heaves not with a sigh,
To see in this neglected spot
 The first of Scotland's heroes lie.

His honour'd, famed, and favourite son,
 Wha boldly did assert her right;
The glorious deeds that he has done
 Deserve a temple's towering height.

When monuments, sae tall an' fair,
 Are rising round on ilka hand,
Has nane a wee bit cairn to spare
 For him that sav'd a sinking land?

Ilk Scot to it will add some stanes,
 Tho' simple, it may be of use,
When freedom wanders Scotia's plains,
 To point the spot where lies her Bruce.

Renowned Bruce! Who rear'd a pile,
 The tide of time shall ne'er o'erturn;
The fabric rais'd 'mang bluid an' toil –
 The cape was laid at Bannockburn.

Tho' some have monuments to boast,
 Their names will never last like yours,
 – It will endure, when their's are lost,
 Amang the rubbish o' their towers.

Thy name on freedom's breastplate stands;
 She for a trophy lang has worn
The chief that led the dauntless bands
 Of Caledon, at Bannockburn.

CHURCHYARD MUSINGS

Is there no date to tell – no note to trace
   How often time has turn'd the circling year,
Since the first corse was carried to this place –
   This hallowed spot – and left to moulder here?

Here untold numbers for long years have slept,
   Oblivion o'er them here its veil has thrown.
Of them on earth no record has been kept,
   Forgetfulness "has marked them for her own."

Here, by the wasted form of feeble age,
   Is laid the man in life's meridian prime:
Both once were actors on this earthly stage,
   But now are lost among the wrecks of time.

Even those who lately spent life's bustling day
   Upon the fields that skirt that crystal stream,
Are now forgot – their memory pass'd away,
   Or coming o'er us like some broken dream.

'Tis still more vain their destiny to scan,
   O'er whose green turf a thousand years have flown;
Their joys and sorrows in life's little span
   Are all forgot, and can no more be known.

Perhaps there are among the slumb'ring dead,
   Some sons of nature, rude and unrefined,
Whose minds were nurtured to a pagan creed,
   That gave no light, but blinder made the blind:

Much polish'd art was far beyond their ken,
   Their only rule was nature's urgent call;
Untried, untutor'd, still they felt as men –
   Life's pains and pleasures come alike to all.

To man's young eye how fair life's morning seems,
   All nature then a smiling aspect wears;
But a few years awake from his dreams,
   By disappointed hopes and thorny cares.

If life is lengthen'd till his vigour cease,
   Until the evening of his days draws nigh,
He often finds his wants and woes increase,
   His path more rugged, and a darker sky.

When years are many, friends are often few –
   They drop like autumn leaves, and leave him lone;
When'er he turns but strangers meet his view –
   A man he knows not, nor to them is known.

In vain to him is earthly stay or trust,
   All dark and dim the evening of his day;
The hearts that loved him are now but dust,
   To him the life of life has pass'd away.

There's few that ever trod the vale of age,
   Where joys departed crowd, a mournful train –
The rich, the poor, the simple, and the great –
   But find, like Israel's king, that life is vain.

Man's guilt has made all earthly objects vain –
   Guilt's made this world a scene of endless strife –
Made human hearts the abode of bliss and pain,
   And pour'd the wormwood in the cup of life.

The blades of grass above each narrow bed,
   Within the churchyard's bound that rankly grow,
May number not the tears that have been shed,
   From age to age, for those that sleep below.

Are parted spirits in a happier sphere
   Forbid to view the scene they left below,
Or learn the fate of those who once were dear?
   But that's a secret we must die to know.

Sure death is dreadful in the sceptic's sight,
  Who thinks the god-like mind and graceful form,
Both sink alike to nothingness and night;
  That man, when dead, will only feed the worm.

The darkness dense that ancient Egypt knew,
  Was light compared to the deep doleful gloom
That wraps the grave, if this dark creed is true –
  The beasts that perish have a milder doom.

Sad is the task to follow friendship's bier,
  Dark is the world when viewed from friendship's tomb:
If heavenly hope still mingle with the tear,
  The gloom is lighted by the life to come.

The Prince of life and Sovereign of the sky,
  Who here, as man, man's costly ransom paid –
At friend's tomb a tear bedimm'd his eye,
  To see the ruin sin and death had made.

More than a tear he gave to human woe –
  To heal these woes his spotless life was given;
To raised the wretched, by their guilt laid low,
  He rose again to plead their cause in heaven.

Sure as the sun a flood of splendour pours
   At morn, to light the earth and ocean's wave;
Sure as the spring awakes the sleeping flowers,
   His voice shall break the slumbers of the grave.

Then parted friends will meet to part no more;
   No more will tears the cheek of virtue stain —
'Mong all the ransom'd of that happy shore,
   No tongue will say that man was made in vain.

ON THE DEATH OF MR PRINGLE OF CLIFTON

When loud-tongued pomp declares the death of kings
   To camps and courts, and rends the welkin high,
Its weeds of woe appear 'neath stars and strings,
   But often fails to prompt the peasant's sigh.

Unlike the artless grief, heartfelt, sincere,
   That clad each rustic brow in funeral gloom,
Round Pringle's hearse, a much lamented bier,
   And shed a tear on his beloved tomb.

The name and memory of the dead are lost,
   Amidst the mighty wreck of things which were,
As ocean's waves to nothingness are toss'd
   As meteors melted in the viewless air.

Fame's cherish'd names are often stamp'd in blood;
   But the red havoc of ambition's hand,
Is kept in memory, like the storm and flood
   That sweep destruction o'er a happy land,

While the best benefactors of mankind,
   Whose god-like deeds fall noiseless as the dew,
Are often to forgetfulness consign'd –
   Fame writes them not among her favour'd few.

But Pringle's name will need no borrow'd arts,
   To future times his memory to extend;
His epitaph's engraved on grateful hearts –
   The poor man's patron, and his country's friend.

His generous heart in kindness did embrace
   Mankind as bothers, and as kindred blood;
Of every caste and colour of our race
   He strove to cause the universal good.

The haughty mein that marks the vulgar great
   Was not congenial to his manly mind;
When served by honest worth of low estate,
   In him the master and the friend were join'd.

His pity wiped the tear from misery's eye,
   His bounty made the helpless orphan glad;
The homeless wretch would seek his home to die,
   And parting spirits bless him ere they fled.

At that dread bar where none will stand unmoved,
   When the loud trump shakes nature's trembling frame,
Deeds such as these will be by Heaven approved;
   Midst countless myriads – his is lasting fame.

LINES
SUGGESTED BY INCIDENTS FOLLOWING
THE PASSING OF THE REFORM BILL

The crowds are glad since freedom has grown gay,
With her new bonnet lately trimm'd by Grey.
Now female-like, with feathers waving high,
She gads about, and woos the public eye;
Let us observe, in groves or crowded streets,
With what reception this gay goddess meets.
We turn to where yon sign-post hangs on high,
Where "wines and spirits" court the traveller's eye –
Joy's boasted mansion, hostile to despair,
The abode of pleasure, and the bane of care.
But, hark! What means the clamorous debate!
'Tis Boniface contending with his mate.
"Hiccup, hiccup, I will no more be fool'd,
I've been too often with a woman rul'd;
I'll let you see reformers have a soul
'Bove Tory threats or petticoat control.

Hiccup, Hiccup, old Scotland shall be free!
Down with Lord John;★ the noble tar for me!"

– Sure such a sot was ne'er of woman born,
No John for you except John Barleycorn!
He's always bizzing in your empty skull –
A pretty man, forsooth, to get your will!
A ne'er-do-weel, now ten times worse than mad,
To league with Elliott's apron'd, plackless squad,
And leave the shadow of the great Buccleugh –
Your best wing feather: you'll get time to rue.

★Roxburghshire was at this time being contested by Lord John Scott and the
Honourable Captain George (now Admiral) Elliott.

I've heard you pray, when reckoning o'er your pounds,
Your only prayer, 'God bless his lordship's hounds!'
For roving hunters, hungry from the hill,
Ne'er stop to grumble at a lengthen'd bill:
We proved their patience when we had them last –
Ah, days of profit, now for ever past!
And poverty comes on, earth's weightiest curse;
For every ill attends an empty purse.
 No country then to us is worth a feg,
They're all but step-dames when we come to beg;
Fools mar their fortune, then they blame their fate,
Avert your ruin ere it be too late.
To-morrow we expect the noble Scott –
Wave flags of welcome- let him have your vote,
And you shall have a bumper running o'er,
To toast your country".

She paused for answer, great was her surprise –
He only snored, for sleep had closed his eyes.
Sunk in his arm-chair sat our portly host –
A patriot still, but slumbering at his post.

Now turn your eye upon the care-worn priest,
Unskill'd 'mong worldly ills to choose the least.
His mind was wont to leave terrestrial jars
Far, far below, and soar above the stars;
But new-born suffrage, that untoward boon,
Detains him 'neath the glimpses of the moon.
Behold him struggling to put Whigg'ry down,
Because he thinks her hostile to the gown;
He prophesies she'll lend the Church a kick,
He hates and fears her worse than he does Nick.
On every one she growls with angry spite,
Whose fees are ponderous, and whose labour's light;
For ever present this dread spectre seems,
When day is past, she haunts him in his dreams.

He wakes his friends with exclamations loud –
"Ah now they triumph! Blast these plebeian tribes!
Heaven shield my country, that is, tithes and glebes!"
Near by him lies the clerk, in slumber bound,
Who, lull'd by Bacchus still, starts at the sound
Of well-known voice, by him ne'er heard in vain,
And tosses, tumbles, and cuckoo's "Amen."

The hardy yeoman watching o'er his crop,
Whose manly labours are his country's prop,
Respected once might wander o'er his fields,
But now degraded by the power he wields.
Perhaps his landlord honour'd lineage claims,
From Jerviswood's or Fletcher's glorious names,
He propp'd their country when a fearful doom
Hung overhead from tyranny and Rome.
When they were dust, their spirits for a space
Seem'd to remain, and hover o'er their race.
In every cottage of their fair domains,
Their fame was echoed by the simple swains;
Their politics their yeomen own'd with pride,
And caught a leaning to the liberal side.
But now in haste arrives the factor's note,
Whose burden is, "Your landlord's turn'd his coat.
He fears, if Whig artillery come to play,
The tax on bannocks may be swept away;
He craves your aid against a ruthless crew,
Who for the shuttle would depress the plough.
Let bigots talk of conscience and of creeds,
'Tis yours to follow where your landlord leads –
The mob's loud clamour learn to disregard –
Stand for your country – that is, please the laird."
- But half converted, till his eye he cast
Upon these lines – "Your lease is wearing fast:
Would you forgo your father's happy seat?
Think, pause, and ponder, ere it be too late".

Now clear conviction streams through heart and head –
He turns a Tory, learns to con their creed,

Quotes great Montrose, and boasts of Clavers' might,
Shews erring Whigs whatever is is right.
Behold him now in patriotic pride,
So firmly planted by his country's side;
To her he vow'd, for her his pledge he'll keep –
Another Curtius ready for the leap!

Their rough, rude sires, who drew the bright claymore,
And pois'd the spear in restless days of yore,
If they their offspring's dastard movements trace,
Will surely blush for the degenerate race,
When they behold them hug the servile chains,
Imposed on them by Whig and Tory thanes.
When men for gain their independence waive,
They sink themselves below the fetter'd slave;
Though Afric's hapless son's in bonds detain'd,
He's nobler far – his soul is yet unchained.

To see the selfish bearing of the age,
Britannia trembles with a sad presage:
The mighty empires that have pass'd away,
Such symptoms show'd when hast'ning to decay.
Of Greece and Rome, go ask each mould'ring bust,
What laid their country's glory in the dust!
Their soil ne'er ceased to nurse the wise and bold,
But that was bootless – all was bought and sold.
A venal spirit saps a common weal,
When banded foes have fail'd with pointed steel.

Though states may still a gaudy splendour boast,
Yet all that's lofty, all that's noble's lost.
Thus independence fleets from shore to shore,
And once departed, she returns no more;

In every clime, despite the patriot's toils,
She droops and withers on exhausted soils.
'Mid Sabine farms see young Columbia stray,
In all the vigour of youth's early day –
Extended suffrage suits her youthful brow,
But only mocks Europa's wrinkles now.

EPITAPH

On ADAM DAVIDSON, who resided in Morebattle about thirty years ago, and was remarkable for his force of character, manly independence, and strongly displayed love of justice. He was by trade a weaver, and although many years have elapsed since his death, a sacred remembrance of his is still cherished in the district, so that he seems in every respect to have deserved the grateful estimate formed of him by the writer of the Epitaph.

Stop, passenger, this grave deserves a tear,
A village Hampden's manly dust lies here;
Though fortune placed him in a humble state,
Yet nature formed him noble, stamped him great.
His mind was sterling to its inmost core,
And fraught with all the hardihood of yore;
A friend to truth, firm dauntless, and sincere,
When duty called him, then he knew no fear.
He, for the rights of others or his own,
Could bid defiance to a mortal frown.
A friend to justice, free from sordid stains,
His lofty spirit scorned ignoble gains.

A friend to virtue, with the humblest dower;
A foe to vice, though decked with wealth and power.
Sometimes his sterner virtues dimmed the rest,
As rolling waves obscure the ocean's breast.
Though he had foibles, we'll his foibles wave,
And rake no failings from the silent grave.

A TALE OF THE COVENANTERS

Young Allan left his native mountain strand
For toils and danger in a foreign land,
When Scotland's sons for honour fought and bled
In many a field by great Gustavus lead.
To nature Allan owed a stalwart frame,
And ardent mind that glow'd for martial fame.
His daring prowess in each contest hot
Soon brought promotion to the hardy Scot.
O'er the brave host of Sweden's warlike king
In ev'ry conflict, vict'ry spread her wing –
A close attendant on his bright career,
At last, at Lutzen, graced her her hero's bier.
Long Sweden mourn'd that day of deadly strife,
And wept at vict'ry gain'd with such a life.
The martial youth, who gather'd from afar
Round that great master in the art of war,
Now found the soldier's mighty magnet lost,
And wand'ring warriors sought their native coast.

Light is the heart of travellers homeward bound.
Our native home! There's music in the sound.
In ev'ry clime where'er the wanderer strays
The fairest spot's his home of early days.
It lies through life pourtray'd to memr'y view,
And fancy lends it a bewitching hue.
Our native streams and vales and streams impart
The brightest halos round the wand'rer's heart.

.

'Mid vet'ran comrades Allan cross'd the main,
And gladly trod his native soil again;
To his paternal home he bent his course,
Where the dark Annan has her mountain source:
A simple steading girt with moorland dun,
Where long his fathers lived from sire to son;
Where Heaven had bless'd them in their rural state –
Above the lowly but beneath the great.
Here Allan seized his pastoral crook again,
Far from the tumults of the tented plain,
And found contentment in the moorland bower;
But earthly bliss is as fleeting as the flower:
His manly form was still in manhood's prime,
His heart was warm, his hand unstain'd by crime;
Though train'd to act the soldier's rugged part,
He still had saved his morals and his heart.

Years roll'd along, and time's dark gloomy tide
Swept many a heart that loved him from his side;

One friend was left, the brother of his youth,
An honour'd preacher of the Word of Truth –
Revered and loved, the idol of his flock,
Who hung with rapture of the words he spoke.
O'er that dear flock he watch'd with love serene –
Their well-tried friend in every changing scene.
He with the wretched shared his humble wealth –
Their prop in sickness, and their guide in health;
A zealous teacher of that faith sublime
That points the eye beyond the edge of time.
The past'ral charge, to him no downy seat,
But an arena for exertion great –
A field for combat, and a course to run,
Where more than empires would be lost or won.
But soon his godlike labours all were past:
A storm arose, and fiends rode on the blast;

The pastor struck, the flock were scattered wide —
To glut despotic and prelatic pride.
Edwin was from his home and flock exiled,
A hunted wanderer on the mountain wild.
Allan was likewise of his all bereft;
By cruel hand no home for him was left;
Because he had a brother' heart confess'd
In Edwin's need, and shelter'd the distress'd.
In happier days, to rural plenty bred,
Oft at their boards the hungry had been fed;
In life's decline, from hill to hill they move,
With nothing left them but each other's love —

In their distress, by pitying peasants fed,
The rock their shelter, and the heath their bed.
Edwin was passive as the lowly reed
That to the gusts of winter bends its head;
Allan unbending as the stubborn oak
That stands erect amid the tempest's shock,
That, till its lofty head to earth be cast,
Still seems to hurl defiance to the blast.
But Edwin, still unawed by Claver' sword,
Still taught in deserts wild the sacred word.
His heart was proof against terrestrial storms —
He view'd the wrath of men as rage of worms;
His house of prayer, some unfrequented glen,
Lone, wild, and distant from the haunts of men.

One day they met, the watchers high were placed,
Whose views commanded all the neighbouring waste.
Soon Clavers' troops were at short distance seen
Advancing on them with destructive mein:
The trumpet's notes upon the wind were flung,
And all the moorlands with their clamour rung.
Now Edwin's tranquil mind with fears was moved —
Not for himself but for the flock he loved.

While they with troubled looks around him press'd,
In accents tender he the crowd addressed:
"Be ruled by me; avoid the murd'rous strife;
Let not an arm be raised to save our life.
Give not these men of blood the least pretence;
For Jesus' sake forgo even self-defence.

Who with the sword asserts religions claim,
Is but a murderer in religion's name;
Though seas of blood have in her name been spilt,
She mourns the victims, but abhors the guilt.
Religion stands aloof from blood-stain'd fields;
Love, patience, meekness are the arms she wields.
Though we are trampled by tyrannic powers,
We still must pardon – vengeance is not ours;
He who sets limits to the raging wave
Can bound man's wrath – its farthest range the grave;
Oft pitying Heaven is moved with mis'ry's tear,
And checks the oppressor in his mad career.

Thus spake this holy man, his brow serene
And voice as calm as danger had not been,
Then moved away, with feeble step and slow,
To meet the leader of the approaching foe;
His people's safety was his only care –
No mercy for himself he hoped for there.
As he advanced the oath and heartless jeer
Fell more distinct and painful on his ear.
"Shoot the old babbler!" bloody Clavers said;
A musket flashed, and Edwin's with the dead.
That vengeful ball but closed the good man's eye
On scenes of woe; – an evil hour was nigh;
His pitying heart escaped the painful shock
It would have felt to see his slaughter'd flock.
As when the fleecy flocks are struck with fear,
And crowd in circles, when the wolf is near,

So waved the crowd, and shifted to and fro,
And sadly rose the wail of female woe.
As Allan saw his brother reel to earth,
Fix'd grew his gaze, and gasping heaved his breath;
Few were his words, but in indignant mood
His warriors eyed fierce Clavers' men of blood.
Allan soon forms his desperate band
That bear the spear, the matchlock, and the brand.
They had been hunted long o'er hill and glen,
To deserts wild beyond the haunts of men;
Without a crime to mis'ry's brink were driven;
Proscribed on earth, no hope was left but heaven.
Those noble peasants, though adverse to strife,
Were forced to arm and combat for their life;
If they surrender'd, what remained for them
But rack, and tortures, and a death of shame?
But few and ill-equipped was their train;
Even valour's self pronounced resistance vain.
The foe came on with imprecations loud,
And pour'd their volleys through the clust'ring crowd.
They prick'd their steeds to gain the heath-crown'd heights,
And fiercely charged, with sabres glitt'ring bright.
No falt'ring there; but madly onward sped;
Here Allan fought, conspicuous 'bove the rest,
Where danger thicken'd and the foemen prest –
Lies many a bleeding foe around him low,
And Clavers self recoiled from his blow.

Yet Allan's files, though brave, could not withstand
A lengthen'd conflict with their little band.
Into a neighbouring sheepcote they withdrew –
A welcome breastwork to the shatter'd few;
The gateway's guarded with the bristling spear,
To check the warhorse in his dread career;
Although their turf-built barrier was not high,
Who passed o'er it only came to die.

From those without the vengeful shot was shower'd;
From those within incessant volleys pour'd;
The muskets flash, beneath the sulphurous shroud,
Glanced like red lightning in the thunder-cloud.
Thus for a while the Covenanters stood,
Like to a rock 'mid ocean's raging flood:
Unlike to it, they melted fast away;
Each passing moment lessen'd their array.
Till their thinn'd ranks no longer could oppose
The fierce assaults of their surviving foes.

'Twas when the promiscuous slaughter rage around
That Allan fell, transfix'd with many a wound.
The lifeless foemen that around him lay
Bespoke his prowess in that fatal fray.
The conflict pass'd, few were the pris'ners made,
And they had better 'mong the dead been laid,
Who now had pass'd beyond life's troubled span –
Beyond the malice and the reach of man.

EPISTLE TO A REV. FRIEND★

Respected sir, this freedom pray excuse,
List to a simple, but no venal muse,
While, in untutor'd strains, she artless sings,
The transient state of sublunary things;
Who looks on life with philosophic eye,
And sees its geegaws, but must heave the sigh.
The present sinks in time's devouring stream,
The past is but an unconnected dream:
Hence mighty empires from their base are toss'd,
And in the vortex of oblivion lost:
What now remains of Greek or Roman fame,
But mould'ring statues, or a sounding name;
Of those who struggle for their country's good
In servile senates, or on fields of blood,
Or gilded science with a bright'ning ray –
All these like meteors blazed and pass'd away.

A haughty state, that some few years before
Made Europe tremble to her farthest shore,
Now humbled low, of hard won glories shorn,
And prostrate to the bands she held in scorn.
Hard strains and toils ambition's restless son,
But ere the topmost tow'ring twig is won,
The giddy height delirious turns his giddy brain,
He tumbles headlong ne'er to rise again.
Each bloodstain'd tyrant, grim with horrid crimes,
Who shook the world and marr'd its fairest climes,
Devours a while, then sinks to night at last:
We trace their actions as a tempest past.
If these are perilous heights where storms are rife,

★ The Rev. David W. Gordon of Earlston

Turn to the valley of domestic life;
Calm lowly walks, beneath ambition's range,
Yet still there's nothing but perpetual change.
See weeping parents tend to their children's bier,
And helpless orphans wail their loss severe;
The guileless comrades of life's op'ning spring,
That joined in cheerful sports and form'd the ring.
But e'er we climb to life's meridian height,
Oft half their eyes are closed in lasting night.
All things around us hasten to decay,
Nor would we wish this scene to last for aye;
It suits not virtue, that celestial fair,
She seems not here as heaven's peculiar care.
In downy case, see prosp'rous guilt repose,
And goodness, struggling with a weight of woes.

O'ercast with clouds this dark horizon lours,
To clear these doubts the godlike part is yours;
And show to tear-worn eyes a fairer shore,
Where pleasures last, and virtue pines no more;
To pour the balm that sooths the stounds of woe,
A nobler task can generous natures know!
Although the world in these degenerate days,
To different aims, a readier tribute pays,
Oft to the hand that guides destruction's car,
And o'er the nations rolls the storm of war,
Awaits the signal by ambition given,
Then sweeps to dust the noblest works of heaven.
Nor is the man denied his share of fame,
Who teaches arts unworthy of the name,
Light frivolous, made pond'rous by the crime
Of murder'd moments or a waste of time!
From our perverted hearts few plaudits rise,
To them that teach the science of the skies;
Like patients in a fiery fever toss'd,
We love the beverage best that hurts us most.

Since bounteous heaven they powerful tongue doth arm,
With fire to rouse, with eloquence to charm;
To show the truth, in pleasing hues array'd,
And call the passions to her aid;
Through all the flock entrusted to thy care,
Let every member claim an equal share;
To man alone the gospel gladness brings,
To deathless spirits, not to stars nor strings;

For when we to the grave girt pile repair,
The prince and peasant both are equal there.
A few short years, on this ungenial shore,
Thy bright and useful labours will be o'er:
'Tis on the wing, though distant be that day,
That lays the lifeless with thy kindred clay,
To sleep secure in death's dark mansions lone,
Till nature wakes thee with her parting groan;
When the vain transient things of time are o'er,
And all is fix'd and change shall be no more.

LINES
WRITTEN ON VISITING THE GRAVE OF A YOUNG FRIEND★

Though cold in dust this mould'ring frame doth lie,
The gen'rous soul that warm'd it ne'er can die;
The mortal part is all the grave can claim,
It can't imprison pure ethereal flame.
The just, when sever'd from this world of woe,
Receive a kindness from a conquer'd foe;
Death's icy arm, when life's last struggles cease,
Unbars the gates of endless joy and peace;
Yet, such the weakness of our nature here,
Our blind affections pour a bitter tear:
For thee, dear shade, how my sad spirit grieved,
What stounds of anguish in my bosom heave!
When time essays to staunch heart-rending wounds,
Or make their torrents flow in proper bounds,
Surrounding objects stir the slumb'ring smart,
And serve as prompters to the bleeding heart.

When the young bands repair to school at morn,
With lightsome hearts, or gladlier home return,
To spend in guileless sports their cheerful day,
Thy part is vacant in their evening play.
When round the cottage hearth the simple ring
Presents the tribute due to nature's king,
The days and months now part, return to view;
Thy seat is empty, and a sigh's its due;
But here our sorrows find a short repose,

★ It may interest the reader to know, that the young friend was the author's own daughter, who died of croup, at the age of twelve.

While hope exulting triumphs over woes –
The hope, thou join'st in nobler songs of praise,
Where raptured angels lofty anthems raise.
Short gleams of sunshine on a stormy coast,
Soon resignation's soothing powers are lost!
In the frail bosom, still to sense enslaved,
Remembrance runs o'er records deep engraved,
No slight impressions soon to be forgot,
But lasting as the minds on which they're wrote:
When sad, I trace them downward from thy birth,
As circling years disclose thy modest worth;
And as each op'ning virtue rose to view,
I counted hopes that round it fondly grew;
But ah! sad change – of all these joys bereft,
My hopes are wither'd, and my wishes left!
How vain's our transient day beneath the sun,
With sorrows clouded ere it's well begun –
Although the time that form'd thy span was brief,
In it you 'scaped not from your share of grief.

It was your lot the bitter tear to spend
O'er the last sufferings of a dying friend,
Which heave the darkest, weightiest wave of woe,
The sharpest pang that generous bosoms know;
And ere that tear was from thy cheek removed,
Down to the grave you follow'd him you loved.
How lost to reason every grief appears
That mourns thy exit from a land of tears;
Are they less bless'd to whom Heaven may ordain

The swiftest passage o'er a stormy main?
The fairest worth first leaves the shores of time,
'Tis not a native of this wintry clime;
It shines a while to draw our wond'ring eyes,
Then wings its way to join its kindred skies;
The brightest worth is lightly prized below,
Till once it's gone, or when about to go;
In dark distress it brightens still more bright,
As meteors blaze throughout the shades of night.
When in the grasp of life's terrific foe,
You bade farewell to all your friends below,
With resignation taught us how to die,
And breathed on earth the temper of the sky:
Thy gentle heart, with death's dark gulf in view,
Possess'd a firmness heroes never knew,
Whom pride impels to tempt the dreary vale,
That awful pass where finite natures fail;
Whate'er their deeds to thoughtless men may seem,
They're no less frantic than a madman's dream.

At the decisive, final, trying hour,
When vain's the aidance of created power,
You lean'd on Him whose arm can succour yield,
Who doth the keys of death's dark mansions wield;
Whose strong right hand, omnipotent to save,
Dispels the terrors that begird the grave;
Streaks death's dark valley with celestial light,
And shields his friends with uncreated might –
Commands the storms which toss the dread abyss,
To waft them smoothly to the climes of bliss.
Such honours grace the exit of the just,
Nor shall the grave detain their sacred dust;
New glories wait them at the drama's close,
When planets drop, and suns their lustre lose.

THE BEGGAR'S ACCOUNT OF HIMSELF

December's rough and surly gust
   Was raving round the leafless tree,
And Boreas, mounted on the blast,
   Was sweeping wild the wintry lea.

I met a man whose aged form
   Was bent beneath a load of years,
Still warsling with the ruthless storm –
   His cheeks were pale and wet with tears.

I said, my sire, you are to blame,
   It surely ill befits your age –
Your faded, weak, and feeble frame
   Will sink beneath the winter's rage.

No home have I, the sage replies,
   From door to door I beg my bread;
No shelter from the angry skies
   That beat upon my houseless head.

I saw the morning sweet, serene,
   I heard at noon the tempest rave;
In life lies many a changeful scene
   Betwixt the cradle and the grave.

Life's morn is big wi' budding joys,
   Right fair the vernal blossoms blaw,
But when the noon-day blasts arise,
   How quick our cluster'd comforts fa'!

Free frae care and canker'd ways,
  Near where the Grampian summits rise,
I spent my cheerful early days,
  In happy, though in humble guise.

The hours flew swift wi' eagle speed,
  And joyless days came in their room,
And every year that did succeed
  Still deepen'd to a darker gloom.

I early lost a faithful wife;
  Six stately sons she rear'd to me,
And saw them in the bloom of life,
  Ere death in darkness closed her e'e.

Four of them fell in distant lands,
  No friendly hand their eyes to close;
They fought among the plaided bands,
  The proudest ranks that Scotland knows,

To sooth my grief and smooth my care,
  My other sons with kindness strove;
The gloomy brow of dark despair
  Was brighten'd oft with filial love.

We rented long a little spot,
  Which fell'd our wants and foster'd health;
Contented in a homely cot,
  Midway 'tween poverty and wealth.

At the restless call of fate,
  Our gen'rous master breathed his last;
Another heir'd his braw estate,
  Whose mind was of a different cast.

74

No spark o' pity warm'd his breast;
   His heart ne'er wi' emotion glow'd;
And a' his passions seem'd to rest,
   Except a sordid thirst o' gowd.

The tenants o' his wide domains
   Were from their homes by av'rice chases;
Some stately tyrants from the plains
   Stalk'd on the desolated waste.

My sons, to independence bred,
   For her, at home, now sought in vain;
They then resolved to seek a shed
   In climes beyond the western main.

But I had tint my youthfu' fire,
   My bluid was cauld, my cheek was wan;
I only had ae strong desire,
   To end my life where it began.

Darkly gloom'd the dowie day;
   We thought to leave our native shore;
To the churchyard I took my way,
   To visit friends that were no more.

My bosom rose with heaving swell,
   My aching heart was like to burst,
I frantic took my last farewell,
   And named the silent sleeping dust.

While throught the darksome aisle I peep'd,
   Where all our parted chieftains lay,
I thought their dusty statues wept
   To see us pass in crowds away.

We'd scarcely left our native shore
  When stormy winds began to sweep;
A tempest rose, whose madd'ning roar
  To fury roused the foaming deep.

We struck upon a deadly rock,
  Then shrill arose a plaintive wail;
Wild o'er our bark the billows broke,
  The stoutest hearts began to fail.

My sons conveyed me to the boat,
  Then went to bring our little store;
Bt ah! It was my wretched lot
  That I should ne'er behold them more.

My breast did with impatience burn,
  I raved, distracted at their stay;
For long before they could return,
  The crowded boat was under way.

And all that to the wreck adhered,
  Were buried deep in watery graves;
For soon the vessel disappear'd,
  Engulph'd beneath the roaring waves.

With grief grown frantic and deranged,
  Insensible I reach'd the strand;
But ah, alas! How sadly changed!
  To me it was a foreign land.

I gazed upon the raging sea,
  With heart as cauld as only stane;
Like to a blasted, leafless tree,
  With a' its spreading branches gane.

The wintry cold my frame benumbs,
  I wander helpless o'er the land,
Depending on the scanty crumbs
  Which fa' from pity's palsied hand.

When oft I shed the bitter tear,
  And sair wi' wants and waes opprest,
It soothes my heart to think I'm near
  That country where the weary rest.

A MOTHER'S LAMENT
FOR THE DEATH OF AN INFANT SON★

Nor tongue nor pen can paint a mother's woes,
When, o'er her infant's eyes, death's shadows close,
With frantic gaze she lingers, loath to part,
And thus, in broken accents, pours her heart;
Adieu my much loved babe, a long adieu
To all the fleeting joys of life and you!
If day's bright orb that, in the heaven, does shine,
And all the regions that he lights were mine,
And could they, from the grave, thy ransom buy,
I'd give them freely as an idle toy.
When thorny cares had wrung my restless breast,
Thy artless smile oft soothed my soul to rest,
And shed more balm upon the wounds of woe
Than ever stoic firmness could bestow.
How pleasing to behold a bosom fair,
That ne'er was ruffled with corroding care;
A guileless face that knew no hollow art
To wear a smile when malice filled the heart.

Oft o'er thy face my eye would fondly stray,
To see infantile beauties dimpling play;
In them those bright and nameless tints appear,
Which fancy makes celestial natures wear;
They are her pattern, when her fingers move
To draw the portraits of the bless'd above.
Anticipation led my partial eye
To future scenes where hope's bright regions lie;
Where bliss unbroken, joy unmingled, seems,

★ The deceased was the author's son.

I there indulged in dear delusive dreams.
I saw thee rise to manhood's active day,
When thy kind hand would all my care repay;
And as these shadowy phantoms moved around,
The scene was stretch'd beyond life's narrow bound.
I saw myself laid on the silent bier,
And you, attending, drop the tender tear.
Such are the airy fabrics which we raise,
As blind presumption builds on future days.
But ah, how frail! When every rising gust
That faintly stirs doth sweep them to the dust!
Thy early exit broke my reverie,
And made me shed the bitter tear for thee!
A dark eclipse bedimm'd thy rising sun,
And marr'd thy course ere it was well begun.
So have we seen a tender flower arise
And open fair in beauty's brightest dyes,
Until a vernal storm defaced the day,
When all its fragrance fell to swift decay.

Sweet blooming flower, ye've left this wintry coast
For worlds unknown, yet still ye are not lost;
You are transplanted to a fairer clime,
And safely shelter'd from the blast of time,
Where ye shall bloom, untainted by decay,
Beneath the beams of everlasting day;
And, when this first drear time of sorrow's o'er,
I hope to find you on that blissful shore,
Where sever'd friendship meets no more to part,
Nor sad adieus nor farewells wring the heart!
Midst all the griefs that crowd life's little span,
A heavenward hope sustains the heart of man.
This beam divine doth gild his path below,
And blazes brightest in the night of woe –
From sorrow's brow dispels the darkest gloom,
And sheds a radiance on the dreary tomb.

But what can soothe the sceptic's bosom-wounds,
When he concludes the grave his being bounds?
No cheerful ray his gloomy soul can boast,
Each friend he loses is for ever lost;
No hoped-for bliss repays his present pain,
He drives at random on life's stormy main;
No chart to warn him where couch'd dangers lie;
No pole-star twinkles in his dusky sky;
Nor end nor aim – a sea without a shore –
No peaceful haven when the tempest's o'er –
His feeble bark a while the billow braves,
Then, hopeless, sinks beneath the roaring waves.

ADDRESS TO LIBERTY

Wide as the range of human kind,
  Extend thy sway, sweet liberty!
In every clime the gen'rous mind
  A ready homage yields to thee.

Of noble gen'rous deeds the nurse,
  Thou brightens life in each degree;
Without thee, being is a curse,
  A bitter cup when reft of thee.

When Afric's hapless sons were torn
  From kindred, country, all that's dear;
Aboard the bark, by ruffians borne,
  They wail'd their destiny severe.

They homeward turn'd their eyes in vain,
  When far upon the trackless sea;
In wild despair they shook their chain,
  And sigh'd they name, sweet liberty!

When commerce links far distant shores,
  Fair freedom, thine's a magic charm;
With thy assistance science soars,
  And matchless is the warrior's arm.

As spring calls forth the opening flowers,
  And bids the frost-bound fountains roll,
Thy breath awakes the slumb'ring powers,
  And stirs the ardours of the soul.

Against thy sons, when Xerxes led
  His millions, ranged in deep array,
Thy radiant sword among them spread
  Pale ruin, rout, and wild dismay.

Till in disgust, in after times,
  Thou badst those shores a long adieu,
And took thy flight to western climes,
  Where Roman eagles proudly flew.

But when thou heardst, with great disdain,
  The base degenerate senate's roar,
The godlike Brutus strove in vain
  To stay thee on his native shore.

For thee, the sons of Britain's isle
  Have danger's darkest form defied;
To win thy grace, and share thy smile,
  A Russel and a Sidney died.

Heart-chilling slavery to expel,
  Brave warriors fill'd a bloody urn;
A Douglas fought, a Wallace fell,
  Red ran the stream of Bannockburn.

When Gallia's sons, with loud acclaim,
  Wild started from despotic chains,
Fired in phrenzy at thy name,
  They dyed with blood Europa's plains.

They every badge of bondage tore,
  Wrought deeds of wonder to be free,
But lost thee in the wild uproar,
  And hugg'd a demon dark for thee!

Then thou, fair freedom, didst retire,
   And slav'ry gloom'd a starless night;
Then languid grew their martial fire,
   That blazed no more than mortal height.

The change, simplicity may scan,
   Who vanquish'd nations them outbraved,
With gleam terrific on their van,
   No more thy sword, fair freedom, waved.

Thy artless sons, who urged the chace
   On fields where science never stray'd,
Unknowing of each polish'd grace,
   With arrows arm'd, in furs array'd.

Hold forth base bondage with a dower
   Of splendour, pomp, and pageantry,
They'll proudly spurn the proffer poor,
   And cling to thee sweet Liberty!

No haughty lordlings bend their mind,
   From nature's king their rights they hold,
They lend more lustre to their kind
   Than servile menials deck'd in gold.

Wide as the range of humankind,
   Extend thy sway, sweet Liberty!
In every clime the gen'rous mind
   A willing homage yields to thee.

LINES
ON THE FALLING DOWN OF THE BELL
OF HOWNAM KIRK★

'Twas at the solemn, silent hour
When mortals drop their cares and strife,
When sleep asserts its silken power,
And levels all the lots of life;
Softly the falling waters sung,
Still slept the breeze on hill and shaw,
And dark the midnight shadows hung
Around the skirts of Hownamlaw;
The wandering moon, with radiant gleam,
Shed chequered lustre o'er the dale,
Through cloudless blue, her silver beam
Fell flickering on the banks of Kale.
I gazed upon the shadowy scene,
When full before my startled sight,
An ariel troop, in glittering sheen,
Flew swiftly o'er the distant height.

A sprightly band, in splendour rare,
All mounted high on splendid horse
That seemed to tread the midnight air,
And paw the moonbeams in their course.
Swift as the rapid falcon speeds,
They skimmed o'er Osmont's summit lone;
And, when they moonward turned their steeds,
Their burnish'd trappings brightly shone.
They hover'd round with shouts of glee;
The, with a rushing, eerie sound,
They lighted on a flowery lea,

★ It was believed in the days of langsyne, that the sound of the kirk bell drove all the
uncanny beings from the country.

And, in a ring, their coursers bound.
Then music's mighty spell was heard;
Like autumn leaves the dancers flew;
So light they trod the flowery sward
They left unbrush'd the drops of dew.
I turn'd, I gazed, I shook with fear,
At the unearthly revelry,
As thus a song fell on my ear,
In wildest strains of minstrelsy –

"Centuries have closed their e'e,
Since our last revelry
Fell on this lovely lea,
    Where Kale's meandering,
Though round the great globe we've been,
Yet have we never seen
Streams more clear, hills more green,
    In our wide wandering.

When truth, in reforming days
Shone with refulgent blaze,
Far from the hateful rays,
    In exile we languish'd.
Far from the hateful knell
Of the dread Sabbath-bell,
A while we'll enjoy oursel'-
    Its note is extinguish'd.

Ye spirits who fled from truth,
Come from the sultry south,
Come from the climes of drouth
    Where you've been fated.
Come from the drowsy west,
Where the day sinks to rest,
To haunts ye once loved best,
    And have regretted!

Warlocks come o'er the main,
Witches come in their train,
Silence prevails again
   Ye need not be eerie.
Mounted on twigs of yew,
Sprinkled with kirkyard dew,
Come to the grand review
   Lively and cheerie!

Come from where tempests growl,
And northern oceans roll;
Come from below the pole,
   Wiser than Parry.
Come to this lovely dell,
Practise the dance and spell;
The bellman's without a bell,
   He cannot scare ye!

Come mermaids with scaly tail,
Kelpies come haunt the Kale,
Brownies come ply the flail,
   Start from your slumber;
Leave your cold Lapland grot,
Come to this lovely spot –
The bell, like a broken pot,
   Now lies in lumber!

We heed not the cannon's roar,
We frolic on fields of gore,
Heaps of slain skipping o'er,
   Where watch fires twinkle;
But when the Sabbath-bell
Sends forth its sullen knell,
We soon find our spirits fail
   At its dread tinkle."

The songster ceased, while deaf'ning shouts
    Rose wildly to the welkin high;
But to the shrill unearthly notes
    The echoes durst not make reply.
But soon the noisy mirth was hush'd –
    For loud the cottage watchman crew;
In bustling haste to horse they rush'd,
    And soon were lost in ether blue.

THE ORDINATION

The sun his golden lustre shed,
And made the lonely Cheviot's head
   Bright with his morning ray;
While vapours lingered in the vale
And hid the crystal streams of Kale,
   As with a mantle grey.

The sprightly lark had hail'd the morn,
The linnet answered from the thorn,
   The blackbird from the grove.
Life seemed to them a time of glee,
A scene of joy and revelry –
   A time of peace and love.

Vain man is oft less blest than they,
More restless in his transient day,
   With all his boasted skill;
To reach some future good he strains,
And, when his object he attains,
   There's something wanting still.

Upon an ordination day,
The gathering crowds, upon their way,
   With hasty steps were seen,
True to the tryst that had been set,
To join the crowds already met
   Upon the kirkyard green.

The ploughman from the lowland dales,
The shepherd from the distant fells,
   The cottar from his cot,
And all the various sons of trade,
Had left their crafts, and hither sped,
   To meet upon the spot.

Their numbers more, as legends tell,
Than e'er the sound of Sabbath-bell
   Call'd to the house of prayer.
That day, in every face was seen,
Of those assembled on the green
   A discontented air.

Of pastor, they no more had choice,
Since law had hush'd the public voice,
   And said they must submit;
'Twas vain objections, then, to make,
Since they must for their pastor take
   Whom e'er his Grace thought fit.

The crowd are oft less wise than wight,
And loath to part with public right –
   Their counsel's rash and vain.
Despite of Anna's mandate high,
They were resolved club law to try
   Their freedom to maintain.

In Scotland's rude and restless days,
To wait upon the law's delays,
   Men had but little skill.
From their own hand to seek remeid,
Long time had been their border creed –
   Its spirit lingered still.

A man was there of stalwart frame,
And Nub of Beaumont was the name
   He'd borne for many a day.
Well fitted for the chief command,
A mighty cudgel graced his hand,
   He'd proved in many a fray.

He seem'd as middle age he'd passed,
His visage harden'd by the blast,
   His features stern and high.
His hair and beard were touch'd by time,
But all the fire of youthful prime
   Still sparkled in his eye.

Great zeal for Scotland's kirk he had –
No common zeal, but zeal run mad –
   As frantic as the wind;
And when his hobby-horse got head,
He, scouring off with reckless speed,
   Left common sense behind.

Being seated on a grassy heap,
Where names now long forgotten sleep,
   The crowd all standing by,
He thus began, with uncouth chime,
And croon'd a rugged border rhyme,
   To keep their spirits high :—

"Ye true border men, at the spot where we meet
The dust of our fathers lies under our feet,
They are freed from life's sorrows, its pleasures and pains,
But I hope, with their sons that their spirit remains.
Though their names be forgotten, their numbers are vast
That here have been laid in the years that are past;
And, doubtless, their ashes may rest in this place,
Who fought for the freedom enjoyed by their race.
Who knows but their dust may be slumbering here,
Who 'gainst the proud Romans once brandished a spear?
Or those who stood boldly, on many rude plains,
Contending for freedom 'gainst Saxons and Danes?

Or some who disdain'd under bondage to cower,
And struggled with England and baffled her power?
To know what our fathers have paid for our rights,
We have only to look at these camp-covered heights,
And to think of the life of privation they led,
With the sky for their curtain, the turf for their bed.
When worsted by numbers, their dwellings in flame,
A camp all the home that their fortune could claim,
Their flocks swept away, and their harvests defaced,
Their country deserted, by foemen laid waste,
Yet, still they persisted in liberty's strife,

When little was left but their swords and their life.
But of all the oppressors our country did know,
Some ones of her princes were worse than her foe.
A tyrant the limbs of his subjects may bind,
But Stuart attempted to fetter their mind.
Though true, loyal subjects, he doom'd them to bleed,
Because they, in conscience, rejected his creed.
Tormented, and hunted, and driven by power
To lodge with the wild beasts on mountain and moor,
To perish with hunger, or be butchered when found
By the bloodhounds of Clavers for murder renown'd.
On fields, when the fury of battle is spent,
The heart of the victor may often relent,
And succour the vanquish'd his hand had brought low;
But the breast of this bigot no pity did know.
Still true to a maxim experience has found –
'No tyranny's safe while religion's unbound,'

For many long year was their sorrow prolong'd;
The scaffolds were wet, and the dungeons were throng'd;
They were still unconquer'd, their tyrants might see;
Though their limbs were in fetters, their spirits were free.
The tyrant, thus baffled, exhausted his day,
By the frown of a nation was frighten'd away,
And freedom again came to gladden our isle,
But high was the price that was paid for her smile.
By the blood of our fathers the boon was achieved,
And liberty they to their offspring bequeath'd.
But in the conveyance entail has no place;
It needs to be guarded by race after race.
Our time has arrived, and the freedom we boast
Must now be defended, or else it is lost.
A vote for our pastor we now are denied;
Our suffrage is mock'd, our remonstrance defied;
We now must make welcome whoever is sent,

Be passive and mute as the flocks on the bent.
For this foul encroachment our clergy we blame –
Their great predecessors, how different from them!
Ne'er tempted by lucre, nor scar'd by a frown,
The rights of the people they counted their own.
The times now are alter'd. There's none to contend
On the side of the peasant, his rights to defend.
Since now on ourselves our dependence must be,
I hope we dare venture a blow to be free.
Be men and stand by me ; If right is bereft,
This day they shall find that our cudgels are left."

So soon as Nubie's rhyme was done,
The door was forced, the kirk was won,
    And fill'd with old and young,
Who all declared, 'midst loud applause,
That they would now defend the cause
    While they could wield a rung.

With clamour now the kirk resounds,
Each lifts his voice, and sense confounds.
    What a sad change is there!
These men once thought it deadly sin
That sacred pile to enter in,
    But with a reverend air.

The kirk was then revered, I ween;
She in broad Scotland sat a queen,
    By Scotland's favour graced.
But now in this unhappy hour,
Dropp'd from her diadem a flower
    That's never been replaced.

The rev'rend party were at hand,
And, at their back, a motley band
   Collected as a guard –
Supposing there might be a fray,
Knowing the rev'rence was away
   They formerly had shared.

They little trust put in the guards,
That day new raised by country lairds,
   To help to back the laws.
Some served for favour, some for pay,
And some were there, in that array,
   Not friendly to the cause.

As to the kirk they pass'd along,
They found it was no friendly throng
   That rudely press'd around.
Now, in the midst of Nubie's corps,
Where kents and collies kept the door,
   No entrance could be found.

With accents mild, and quiet mien,
They now resolved, upon the green,
   Their duties to perform.
They thought that mildness might allay
The stormy spirit of the day,
   And dissipate the storm.

They begg'd them to the laws to yield,
And not to make a battle-field
   Above the peaceful grave.
But they a hearing were denied,
They might as well with words have tried
   To lull the stormy wave.

A rev'rend brother from the Tweed
Began credentials then to read,
   Obedience to command.
Before his eye a line could trace,
A Jenny Geddes of the place
   Had snatch'd it from his hand.

A country laird who came to head
The law's supporters, now with speed
   To seize the carline flew;
But Nubie's bands who were not slack,
And only waited the attack,
   Rush'd on to the rescue.

Full hot the combat did begin,
And cudgels met with rattling din,
   And all was wild uproar;
The clamour rang o'er hill and dale,
And woke the echoes of the Kale,
   That long had slept before.

Full stoutly was the fight maintain'd,
And ground was lost, and ground was gain'd ;
    But, when they backward trod,
Their heads to save from cudgel wheels,
The grassy hillocks tripp'd their heels,
    And laid them on the sod.

This was a fight where none were slain,
For, in short while, they rose again
    And mixed in the affray;
And long the conflict might have burn'd,
Had not a band, like Bruce's, turn'd
    The fortune of the day.

Maids, wives and widows were the band,
Who nobly then, with heart and hand,
    On Nubie's side fought keen;
 Nor did they ammunition lack –
The kirkyard dyke was at their back –
    They found a magazine.

When, in the front they did descry
Fierce Nubie's cudgel waving high
    A signal now to close;
At last they did the rear assail,
And showers of flints, as thick as hail,
    They hurl'd among their foes.

A favourite follower of the laird,
That day a great man in the guard,
    Now proudly made his boast:
"Come on, ye brave, and follow me,
We now must check the archery,
    Or else the day is lost."

A chosen party at his back,
He boldly marched to the attack,
    With fierce and furious mien:
But, while he brandished round his rung,
A stone by a stout carlin flung,
    Soon stretched him on the green.

His party thought their leader slain,
But in short while he rose again,
    Not deadly was the wound;
But after that, his distance kept
From where that rude artillery swept,
    And fought on safer ground.

The clergy now bewail'd the day,
But had no power to quell the fray,
    Since blood was hot and high.
They stood, like cravens on the spot,
And often jouked a random shot,
    As stones flew whistling by.

The guards could now no longer bear
Those fierce assaults on front and rear,
   Though little blood was shed;
But when they saw Nub leading on
Another charge, with stick and stone,
   They wavered, reel'd and fled.

The clergy also left the field,
Their sacred calling was the shield
   That day that saved them still;
But many thought that, from the fray,
They had not gone so safe away,
   If Nub had got his will.

The victors had no cause to toss
Their bonnets high – they'd gain'd a loss,
   Like Pat who won the plea.
For many were to prison haul'd,
When broken laws for vengeance call'd
   On that day's revelry.

They now perceived the thought was vain,
Rights to acquire, or to retain,
   By reckless deeds of strife;
For, right or wrong, the law prevail'd,
The presentee was there install'd,
   Their minister for life.

Although the living he had got,
It seemed, when viewed, no envied lot,
   From what had pass'd before;
But, like a bark, forced by the blast
And stormy sea, had anchor cast
   Upon a hostile shore.

A man he was of mildest mood,
Who still for evil render'd good,
   And strife desired to shun.
When evil tongues were loud in strife,
He answer'd only by his life
   And duties kindly done.

When feuds at first against him rose,
His mildness oft disarm'd his foes
   His kindness friends increased –
As sleeping winds, and skies serene,
Can soothe the tempest troubled main,
   And smoothe her wat'ry breast.

When he depicted sinners' strife,
The tenor of his blameless life
   But by it brighter shone.
When by the Scripture model true,
He the meek Christian's likeness drew,
   The portrait was his own.

A friend to man of every hue,
The poor man's friend, whose friends are few –
   Distinctions he made none.
To all he gave a parent's hand,
To guide unto a happier land
   Where want and woe's unknown.

Though short his date, before its close
He found he had outliv'd his foes;
   Even Nub the hand extends,
And many, foremost in the fray,
On his rude ordination day,
   Had now become his friends.

He lived respected and beloved –
But worth is, often, soon removed –
   At least, we think it so.
Long, long, upon his narrow bed,
Were bitter tears sincerely shed
   For him that slept below.

The good man's life doth still proclaim
That virtue's not an empty name;
   For, man of gen'rous worth,
Howe'er his path of life may be,
Though poorly low, or proudly high,
   Has still reward on earth.

ANNA AND MALCOLM

Anna of Benmore long followed her Malcolm,
    And often the battle saw through the salt tears;
Although to herself every fortune was welcome,
    She fear'd no privations if Malcolm was near.

He fought under Moore, when misfortune was low'ring;
    With him she travers'd the stern mountains of Spain;
But hardship and famine her frame overpowering,
    She sunk 'neath the toils of that hapless campaign.

Stretch'd over the cold sward, the army was lying,
    Each worn, weary soldier reclining his head,
When Malcolm stole softly, with sorrow and sighing,
    To make, for his Anna, her dark narrow bed.

'Twas night, and the wild blast of winter was scowling;
    The foeman's shrill bugle was heard from afar;
Upon the lone mountains, the grim wolf was howling,
    At distance, still dogging the footsteps of war.

The sharp throb of anguish the salt drops was draining,
    When soft on her bosom the damp turf he laid;
Her young son she'd left him, lay by him complaining,
    All wretched and helpless, wrapt up in his plaid.

With tender emotion his bosom was swelling:
    So dark is the death-scene of those whom we love,
To cast a lone look on their dark narrow dwelling,
    Shakes hearts which the thunder of war cannot move.

His young son he clasps with redoubled affection,
    As back to his comrades bewilder'd he strays;
But seems as detained by some powerful attraction –
    He lingers, retires and again turns to gaze.

He carried the infant, with sorrow assaulted,
    'Mid thick crowded columns, in peril and pain;
On the field of Corunna, a short time they halted,
    Before it was soak'd with the blood of the slain.

Around them the armies of Gaul were a-thick'ning;
    His son on his shoulders he fasten'd with care;
Before them, the dark cloud of battle was black'ning;
    His mates of the mountain for conflict prepare.

The shot-shiver'd banner which over them wav'd,
    Whilst their's was the calmness that confidence yields ;
The scars on their features with toil deep engraved,
    All showed them no strangers to hard foughten fields.

The number of foemen was hourly increasing;
    From steel-cover'd squadrons the flashing blaze shone,
Concenter'd and marshall'd, and vanward still pressing,
    Till England's loud bugle the battle call'd on.

The hoarse-sounding pibroch old Scotland's sons cheered,
　　When almost obscured 'neath the sulph'rous shade;
Through dark, rolling vapour but dimly appeared
　　The nod of the bonnet and wave of the plaid.

The legions, tho' laurell'd, unused to such welcome,
　　Confounded, astonish'd and shatter'd, recoil;
In the moment of vict'ry, unfortunate Malcolm
　　Was struck by a death-shot, and sunk on the soil!

With gaze dim and tender, his young son he eyed,
　　Then beckon'd his comrades his young son to save;
His tried mates in danger alertly complied;
　　For pity's loved haunt is the breast of the brave.

"Companions! " he falter'd, "from Malcolm receive him,
　　Unshelter'd and helpless – of kindred bereft—
And, when you return, to your country bequeath him,
　　The last of his race that her battles have left."

ON VISITING THE SCENES OF EARLY DAYS

Ye daisied glens and briery braes,
Haunts of my happy early days,
Where oft I've pu'd the blossom'd slaes
   And flowers fair,
Before my heart was scathed wi' waes
    Or worldly care.

Now recollection's airy train
Shoots through my heart with pleasing pain,
And streamlet, mountain, rock or plain,
   Like friends appear,
That lang, lang lost, now found again,
    Are doubly dear.

But many a dauted object's fled;
Low lies my once paternal shed;
Rank hemlocks wild, and weeds o'erspread
   The ruin'd heap;
Unstirr'd by cheerful tongue or tread
    The echoes sleep.

Yon bonnie burn, whose limpid streams,
When warm'd with summer's glowing beams,
Have often laved my tender limbs,
   When my employ
Was chasing childhood's airy whims
    From joy to joy.

Upon yon green, at gloamin' grey,
I've often join'd in cheerful play,
Wi' comrades guileless, blithe and gay,
    Whose magic art,
Remember'd at this distant day,
    Still warms the heart.

Ah, cronies dear! for ever lost !
Abroad on life's rough ocean toss'd,
By adverse winds and currents cross'd,
    By watching worn,
Some landed on that silent coast,
    Ne'er to return!

Howe'er the path of life may lie,
If poorly low or proudly high,
When scenes of childhood meet our eye,
    Their charms we own,
And yield the tribute of a sigh
    To days long gone.

TO THE SHADE OF WALLACE

Hero of Ellerslie! thy unshaken soul,
Nor threats could awe, nor tyrants could control;
Each manly bosom yields a fond applause
To thee, great champion! bold in freedom's cause!
While mighty nobles, high in birth and power,
For sook their country in her darkest hour;
Proud of the blood that circled in their veins,
Yet basely slumber'd in ignoble chains;
Indignant, then you drew the vengeful sword,
'Gainst mighty England and her haughty lord,
With firm resolve your country dear to save,
And rather perish than become a slave.

Five hundred years have bid the world farewell,
Since thou, a martyr, for thy country fell;
Though no neglect can dim thy deathless fame,
Yet Scotland owes a statue to thy name!

With lavish hand, she squanders wealth away,
On insect names, that scarce will last a day;
Whom fate has doom'd in darkness drear to rot,
For, ere their pile's complete, their name's forgot;
Till one arose, of genius taste, and birth,
And nobly dared to honour parted worth;
With generous hand, thy mimic form uprears,
Where Caledon and freedom mingle tears.

Renowned Shade, on Caledonia smile,
For her thou struggled long, with glorious toil;
May thy unconquer'd fire, while ages run,
Glow in the bosom of her latest son!
Should independence from our country fly,
And love of her in British bosoms die;
Should Scotland mourn amidst her patriots' graves,
And her rough mountains turn the haunts of slaves;
Then, even then, thy gen'rous worth, sublime,
Can ne'er be tarnish'd with the rust of time,
But will shine forth, in unextinguish'd fame,
While there's a heart that warms at freedom's name.

WALLACE'S FAREWELL

Adieu to the land that my fathers defended,
  The land of the warrior, untrod by the slave;
The land of proud hearts, whom a tyrant ne'er bended,
  The loved haunt of freedom, the nurse of the brave!
Alas! I am destined to leave thee for ever,
  From kindred and country by treachery torn;
When prowess has fail'd, now fraud has prevailed,
  Like a felon in fetters, to ruin I'm borne.

I scorned the path of the lawless aggressor,
  Whose boundless ambition all limits defy;
My heart's dearest meed was to curb the oppressor,
  And to wipe the salt pearl from Liberty's eye:
Such were the objects that kindled my ardour,
  But war I abhorred, with its wild, wasting train;
When vict'ry had smiled and slav'ry recoiled,
  I glow'd for my country, but sigh'd for the slain.

Famed heroes!   ye shades of companions undaunted !
  Who fell in the combat our country to save;
I envy your exit, by fetters untainted –
  To perish for freedom's the boon of the brave.
Ye warriors I've led, who still live for your country,
  And stride in the van of her warlike array,
My ruin will warm you, my wrongs, they will arm you!
  And whet the red weapon on battle's rough day.

Let not the proud spoiler exult when I'm taken
   And dash'd by deceit from the pathway of fame;
Although a lone captive, my spirit's unshaken –
   His racks and his dungeons shall find me the same!
Adieu, my dear country, my last look shall linger,
   Until your bleak mountains are lost to my view;
I've left you a dowry of daring and glory,
   That tyranny never can sever from you!

ON HEARING THAT A MONUMENT WAS BEING ERECTED IN MEMORY OF ROBERT BURNS

Pledge to the hearts! Joy be their lot!
    Who bid the sculptured column rise,
To mark the sacred, honour'd spot,
    Where Coila's deathless poet lies!

In memory of the matchless bard,
    Who in the vale of poortith pined:
Though fame bestows a great reward,
    Too late to him his country's kind.

 In fame's fair roll, a radiant blaze
    Encircles his immortal name –
A monument, to latest days
    Of Scotland's glory and her shame.

She's now exulting in his lays,
    His soothing, witching, magic strain;
Each tongue is lavish in his praise –
    Like Scotsmen, wise when wisdom's vain.

Misfortune with perpetual howl,
    Involved him round in starless night,
And chill'd the ardours of his soul,
    And damped his fancy's towering flight.

When on the couch of anguish laid –
    His manly spirit sick'ning low –
He look'd in vain for friendly aid,
    To soothe the pangs of want and woe.

While av'rice, with unpitying eye,
    And rocky bosom, flinty hard,
Half blushing at such apathy,
    Now blames the follies of the bard.

The ardours of his vig'rous mind,
    Might tempt from sober paths to stray;
His tender feelings, too refined
    For life's rough, rugged, thorny way.

When sore bestirr'd, the gen'rous steed
    Bounds reinless, wild, and scours the heath,
While the dull ass, with tentie heed,
    Still jogs along the beaten path.

Not that I would fair virtue slight,
    The prince of Scotia's bards to praise;
Though I adore his genius bright,
    I mourn his ill directed lays.

TO A WATER-FOWL

Capering in maternal pride,
On the dimpling pool ye ride,
Wi' your offspring by your side,
    Blythe sportin' round;
No thought o' what may e'er betide
    Your peace can wound.

But soon the union will be broke,
That binds this little friendly flock;
Some doom'd to perish by the stroke
    O' beasts o' prey
An' ruthless man, wi' heart like rock,
    More fierce than they.

But transient are thy bosom's throes,
For thine are only short-liv'd woes;
Thy heart when torn will quickly close,
    No scars remain,
While from the power of memory flows
    Lang ling'ring pain.

When peace the human heart forsakes,
The vacant room pale mis'ry takes,
Tho' lull'd by time, she oft awakes;
    Each dread review,
That restless power, Remembrance, makes
    She starts anew.

To look on thee, man weel may trace
An emblem o' his hapless race,
That in life's morn, wi' cheerfu' face
   Aroun' him play;
Unconscious that destroyers base
   Lurk in the way.

A few short years o' joy an' glee,
Flee round below a parent's e'e,
Then, launch'd upon life's stormy sea
   Where tempests roar,
Their friendly barks asunder flee
   To meet no more.

THE AULD SOGER

The morning sun the mist was scatterin',
 On the banks o' Tweed sae fair,
When on the way I met a vet'ran,
 Limpin slow wi' pensive air.

Wi' curious e'e his face I tented,
 That ance had seen some better times,
I found his cheek was deeply painted
 In the hue o' warmer climes.

Altho' his head was turning hoary,
 Still his features spake the man;
I asked him to relate his story;
 He sat him down, and thus began:

"Near to yon spot, where Tweed's meand'ring,
 First I drew the vital air,
Sin' syne I've passed a life o' wand'ring,
 Mixed wi' peril, toil an' care.

"When youthfu' bluid, w' rapid motion,
 In my veins did briskly run,
I left this isle, and crossed the ocean,
 To bask in India's burning sun.

"Could I relate, in mournfu' ditty.
 What Britons fand untimely graves;
Or tell how oft I saw, wi' pity,
 The suf'rings o' that land o' slaves.

"With cheerful hearts the waves we breasted,
   Back to Britain's healthsome isle,
Tho' glad to see't, short while we rested;
   They sent us to the banks o' Nile,

"Where the wale o' Bonny's bruisers
   Struggles hard – but forced to yield
To see the lads in tartan trowsers,
   Kenn'd in many a bluidy field.

"Owre Spain's steep hills wi' Moore I march'd,
   Shivering in December's frost,
Upon our van sat famine perch'd –
   And rearward was a num'rous host.

"I was where Britain's trumpet sounded
   The onset on Corunna's plain;
I lost an arm, this leg was wounded,
   Near the spot where Moore was slain.

"Wi' age an' wounds unfit for serving,
   Frae the army I'm dismiss'd;
Yet I am secured from starving,
   Safely stow'd in Chelsea's list.

"How blythe I was to see my country
   To describe I want a tongue,
Tho' into her I made my entry,
   Lam'd an' hirpling o'er a rung.

"I had a wish, tho' now its blasted,
 It cheer'd me oft when far away,
To spend 'mang friends, wi toils exhausted,
 The gloamin' o' life's weary day.

"But oft we see our hopes expiring;
 O' that comfort I'm bereft,
For all my friends I've been inquiring,
 But none of a' my race is left.

"Amang you shrubs, by nature planted,
 My father's ruined cottage stands,
Its image oft my bosom haunted,
 Far frae hame, in foreign lands.

"I view'd it lang wi' sighs an' sobbing,
 Leanin' o'er the ruined wa';
Sic pulses to my heart gaed throbbing,
 I thought my breast wad rive in twa.

"I've been unmoved, tho' foes assailed me,
 When ranks were closing furiously,
But here my wonted firmness failed me,
 The tear fell from a sogers's e'e.

"As round ilk weel-kenn'd haunt I dander'd,
 The days of auld passed in review,
I marked the spots where oft I wander'd,
 When life and a' its joys were new.

"When hearts were light as ony feather,
   Free from sorrow, care and strife,
Before the clouds began to gather,
   That dim the noontide sky of life.

"A fop came to me richly dress'd,
   In a' the splendour India yields,
He roughly thus himself express'd,
   'Begone, ye vagrant, off my fields!'

"Wi' grief, before, maist broken-hearted,
   I e'ed him o'er wi' great disdain;
To catch my sword, this stump oft started,
   But hand and sword were left in Spain."

LINES WRITTEN ON CHEVIOT

Renowned Cheviot! Scotia's southern bound,
Whose lofty head looks down on glens profound, –
Glens set about with pond'rous rocks sublime,
That scorn the rage of torrents and of time.
The mountain's breast is mark'd with many a scar,
Torn in the strife of elemental war.
Here, tow'ring cliffs erect their hideous form,
Where sits enthron'd the genius of the storm.
Here, lofty peaks of proud gigantic height
Do cleave the clouds, amidst their rapid flight,
Whose heads are gilded with the earliest ray,
And the last glimmering of the parting day.
When Spring drives Winter from the fertile plains,
He here entrenched, a while his sway maintains,
Where oft he can the sultry heats defy,
Hid from the glance of summer's beaming eye.
How poor the pigmy strokes that art can boast!
The mind is here in admiration lost.

Each object that appears is great and grand,
Here nature labours with a giant hand.
This once the theatre was of loud alarms,
Where Douglas an' fierce Hotspur met in arms;
Two chiefs Brittania proudly gloried in,
Whose names have often swell'd the battle's din.

LINES WRITTEN ON DECEMBER

December chill doth now advance,
  An' strews the fells wi' whitening frost,
While Phoebus gi'es a distant glance,
  Like faithless friends, when wanted most.

The beauteous landscape's now defaced,
  The fields look cheerless, bleak an' bare,
The eye looks languid o'er the waste,
  All nature wears a pensive air.

No more the blythsome lark we hear,
  Save when in pensive strains he grieves;
The red-breast mourns the aged year,
  Amidst a shower of falling leaves.

The plover's plaintive, wailing cries,
  Ring dreary o'er the lonely fells,
As he in airy circles flies
  Out o'er the faded heather bells.

No more the lovely daisy grows,
  The woodlands mourn their leafless sons;
Now stripped to the naked boughs
  To shun the brizz o' winter's win's.

The pines still keep their wonted hue,
  And rear aloft their stately forms,
An emblem of the glorious few
  Who stand unchang'd 'mid threat'ning storms.

EPISTLE TO WILLIAM BENNET

The lee lang day fatigued and toil'd,
Wi' to the haunches soil'd,
   Thrang delvin' in a ditch;
Yet still it's needless to repine,
Though poor's the lot – it's your's and mine;
   We canna a' be rich.

The rich pretend that care and strife
Ne'er haunt the walks of humble life,
   But happiness is sent
On visits to the cottage door,
To cheer the labours of the poor,
   Led on wi' sweet content.

The poor as often throw their eyes
Up to the couch where grandeur lies,
   A-lolling at his ease;
Contrasting with their toil an' care,
His downy nest, an' dainty fare,
   They think the spot might please.

When grandeur's viewed from poortith's vale,
Where chilling damps and fogs prevail,
   We often judge amiss;
The distance cheats the simple wight,
He oft mistakes the glittering sight
   For perfect joy an' bliss.

A nearer view makes us confess,
The means of human happiness
   Are very equal shared;
For, when we right consider a',
We find the differ is but sma'
   'Tween cottars and the laird.

We see the tall an' lofty oak
Is most exposed to the shock,
   When Boreas shows his ire;
What time the shrub, whose lowly form
Escapes the raging of the storm
   Is trampled in the mire.

Dame nature with impartial hand,
In ev'ry clime, an' ev'ry land,
   An equal blessing throws
Among her sons, wher'er they're bred,
In lordly ha', or lowly shed,
   In spite o' fortunes nose.

When stern misfortune bends her bow,
And aims her shafts at me or you,
   We'll shun what's low an' mean;
Amidst the stour we'll catch content,
And scorn each peevish, poor complaint,
   That ne'er can serve a preen.

Though coward maukin 'mang her faes,
 Skirls loudly out her sang o' waes,
   Wi' dastard crawl an' cringe,
Yet still she meets as hard a doom
As reynard, wha, wi' sturdie gloom,
   Disdains to gie a whinge.

Misfortune, often, follows hard
The luckless creature, ca'd a bard;
   She hates the rhymin' race;
As soon as e'er they touch a quill,
Or glow'ring up to Parnassus hill,
   She marks them for the chase.

She musters up her meagre power,
Some take the field, some slyly cour
   In ambush on their road;
Each aim they take the miss is sure,
Nor are they ever more secure
   Till in below the clod.

There's many ane I've heard confess,
To win content and happiness
   Ye have an unco skill;
For when she turns a wee thought shy,
Or shoars at times to pass ye by,
   Ye bribe her wi' a gill.

Wi' aquavitae's magic power,
Ye charm contentment for an hour,
   Meanwhile ye weet your throat;
But short indeed is oft her stay,
Though e'er sae soon she slips away,
   Her visit's worth a groat.

These wide extremes let us escape,
Where spendthrifts frisk, an' misers scrape,
   Wha's warst let judges tell;
Wi' thoughtless whims an' follies hurl'd,
The one may sometimes wrang the world,
   The other cheats himsel'.

O lust of gowd! The warst of ills,
That e'er the cup of mortals fills,
   For nought but death may cure;
Until our hapless fate be such,
To wear a purse we daurna touch,
   We'll ne'er be truly poor.

As soon's a despot wins a throne,
His black prescriptions hurry on
    The patriot's blood to shed;
So avarice, in the human soul,
Can never reign without control,
    Till every virtue's fled.

The aged, crush'd wi' wants an' years,
The widows', and the orphans' tears
    Make gen'rous bosoms melt;
The god-like thrills that softly roll
The tide of pity o'er the soul,
    By him are never felt.

The muse oft wi' the miser vext,
Will sometimes wander off her text
    To win at him a fleg;
While her citation wants the force
To reach that tender part, his purse,
    He disna care a feg.

The miser's core ye ne'er was in,
To them you're neither kith nor kin,
    I'll freely pass my word;
And when that ye are dead and gane,
None needs to write upon your stane,
    This world has tint a herd.

For heedless an' dreadless,
    O' days ye may never see,
Ye watch aye an' catch aye
    The moments as they flee.

RELIGION VERSUS SECT

Naught but the Christian's faith, celestial light,
Bewildered man can lead through error's night,
In peaceful paths, till happier worlds appear,
Or soothe his troubles while a wanderer here.
Such the Religion that the skies have given,
But men have robbed it of the hues of Heaven;
The glorious guest is clothed in worldly weeds
By kings and priests, to suit their various creeds.
When Papal Rome upreared her mitred crest,
Till half the world was prostrate 'neath the priest,
In superstitious thraldom states were held
Which her victorious legions never quell'd;
Low in the dust, the mightiest monarchs knelt,
Till earth was wrapped in darkness to be felt;
The rule of life that to the world was given
Was "Pay the Church, the only path to Heaven".
This mumm'ry bore religion's sacred name,
The arguments were gibbets, racks and flame;

But when the rays of reason beam'd abroad,
 The nations cast their sacerdotal load;
Then the loud war-note rung from coast to coast,
"The Church in danger, and Religion lost!"
But these were days of darkness, passed away,
Now reason reigns and poured a bright'ning ray.
Religion shows credentials from above,
In teaching men peace, charity and love;
So churchmen tell, but mark your boist'rous scene,
Where death-shots hiss upon the village green.
'Tis the true church, engaged in mortal fray
With stubborn peasants, that refuse to pay
For ghostly counsel that was never given,
And now they're slaughtered in the name of heaven.

The parson, still tenacious of his hire
He never earn'd, approves the murd'rous fire,
 By orphans' cries and widows' moans unmoved,
 When wailing o'er the mangled forms they loved.
The mercy sighs, and pity drops a tear,
And reason thinks there's no religion here.

Is true religion found with Calvin's creed?
In that rough mountain land beyond the Tweed,
With dewy tears, where desert wildflowers weep
On the bleak moorland, where the martyrs sleep,
Whose zeal for truth a despot tried to tame,
By dint of torture and the sword of Grahame,
Till pitying heaven, moved by the sufferers' moan,
Hurled the blood-stained tyrant from the throne.

The patriotic preachers and their flocks
Were worthy of the land of Bruce and Knox,
Firm, unsubdued, tenacious of their right,
Until they triumphed o'er tyrannic might.
Unhappy Stuart, bigoted and blind,
Who madly strove to fetter deathless mind;
But baffled still, despite his savage tools,
Like tigers ruthless but as statesmen fools.
When William wisely sheathed the bigot's sword,
Men's native rights were, then, in part restored,
No more the oppressor on the peasant trod,
And, without terror, men could worship God;
Not in the mode prescribed by mitred pride,
But free to follow Scripture for their guide.
Though Laud's dark spirits stalk in sullen mood,
Yet bigotry no longer fed on blood.
When blest with freedom, various sects arose,

Who viewed each other with the eye of foes;
The many creeds were scriptural, the same,
And all their differences but an empty name, –
A name which proved to many cause of spleen,
Kept man from man, as gulfs were fix'd between.

The numbers few, that think or act alone,
Men often move, as leaders wave them on.
In former days, even pastors have been known
To preach all parties erring but their own.
O'er Christian kindness breathed a chilling frost,
And for a shadow was the substance lost.

We hail the dawning of a happier day,
When bigotry is sinking into decay,
When education aids the mental sight,
 Amidst the blaze of revelation's light,
Candid to read that volume from above,
That teaches peace, good will, and Christian love.

EPITAPHS

Below this turf, Wat o' Wimperton lies,
A man whom the world deemed prudent and wise;
He ne'er was an Atheist, his god was his purse,
His interest the magnet that ruled his course;
To steer by this pole-star he ne'er did neglect,
He veer'd, wheel'd, and wimpled as it did direct.
When chafed wi' bodies o' humble degree,
His fury ran wild as the waves of the sea,
When the roar o' the tempest hath roused the floods;
But who can be pester'd wi' poortith and duds!
When pride, wealth and tyranny stamped and bann'd,
 His passion was wind-bound, he cringed and he fawn'd;
But if they were sportive, and aimed at a jest,
Though distant from wit as the east from the west,
Moved as by magic, he joined in their glee,
Convulsed wi' laughter, folk thought he wad dee.
To deal wi' the gentry he weel kenn'd the knack,
He fawn'd to their face, and he thieved at their back;

†

He never had friends, yet in spite of his foes,
He ne'er wanted langkail, wi' bannocks an' brose.
But O wofu' change! The cauld yird is his bed,
And to the immortals his spirit has fled;
What, there, is his fortune no man can reveal,
But while in this world the bodie did weel.

Here William of Windhope lies under this sod,
A man whom the world thought wilful and odd;
His nature was gen'rous, his judgement was clear,
His feelings were manly, his friendship sincere;
His virtues revered, though in poverty's clutch,
He scorned the worthless, though titled and rich;
He never was skill'd in the world's safe lore, –
To bow to the steed for the trappings it wore.
When misery besought him, his pity o'erflow'd,
If poortith benumb'd him, a sigh he bestow'd.
So feels when in fetters the gen'rous and brave,
To look on the helpless o'erwhelm'd in the wave –
Such notions may do for the land of the leal,
But here, their possessors but seldom do weel.

THE GYPSY'S RANT

The blythesome spring again is seen,
The gowan glents upon the green,
The primrose paints the briery brae,
The milk-white blossom decks the slae;
The sma' bird sings upon the tree,
But naething now brings joy to me:
I've wandered lang and far awa',
I've numbered four score years and twa,
My day is worn to the gloamin' hour,
The dowie night's begun to lour,
Although my calling's counted mean,
I've lived as happy as a queen;
I've tasted a' the joys o' life,
The lover and the happy wife;
And a' the fondness mothers hae –
What's mair enjoyed by ladies gay?
I've often heard the working train
Roose a' employments but their ain;

Wi' them contentment is sae rare,
Just onything but what they are;
Some ither craft they ill could dree,
But that was ne'er the gate wi' me.
 I swear by a' my wand'ring kin!
Had I my life now to begin,
Could I row back the time that's fled,
I still would chuse nae ither trade.
When blinks o' spring had warm'd the sward,
I envied neither lord nor laird;
My heart was light, though busk'd in duds,
Free as the songsters o' the woods;
And, like them, seldom cross'd wi' care,
Ilk day brought me my daily fare.

When summer's burning heats oppress,
When I was weary I could rest;
Cower'd in shade o' shaw or dyke,
I often e'ed the drudgin' bike –
To see them tug and toil sae sair,
I bless'd my lot still mair and mair.
When autumn waved wi' yellow grain,
For me ilk ane might shorn their ain;
Wi' uncraized banes I passed my days,
Though scant o' gear, I still had ease;
But they that winna toil and sweat,
I've oft been tauld they shou'dna eat –
Was this a law through Christendie,
There's mony mae would fast than me.

When wintry spates made sykes to row,
An' storms scowl'd on the Cheviot's brow,
This was the hardest time we kend,
Yet still we fought and made a fend.
Although we hardships underwent,
We wander'd aye wi' backs unbent,
And didna need tae starve our nieves,
Wi' nibblin' neeps frae 'neath the wreaths.
Although we couldna boast a fire,
We lodged right weel in barn or byre;
Stretch'd wi' the hawkies on the hay,
Fu' snug and cozie oft we lay.
Though pride may toss her head aloft,
Our beds by custom seem'd fu' soft;
On custom, puir folk's comfort hings,
It fills the gap 'tween them and kings;
Ambition's gewgaws, when possest,
Can ne'er bring solace to the breast;
A kingly crown to purchase bliss,
Is feckless as my amous dish.
When young, I sometimes tried a knack,

To cheat the crowd, and catch a plack;
The gonyels trow'd that I foresaw
In future days what wad befa';
And, by the dint of magic spell,
I could their fates and fortunes tell;
Whae'er sic senseless stuff believed,
They weel deserved to be deceived.

There's mony a vain and lordly tyke
Thrives by the blindness o' the bike
They fleece them bare, and scorn them baith,
While I could do them little skaith –
I spaed them aye a lucky lot,
And made them happy for a groat.
Now superstition's on the waning,
The day o' reason's at the dawning,
Sin' light's been glimm'ring in ilk noddle,
Nae cantrips now can bring a bodle;
This trade o' mine, like mony mae,
Is rather wearin' down the brae;
There is an unco alteration,
Sin' first I tried this occupation:
What happy langsyne days I've seen!
The commons then lay fair and green;
Oftimes upon their flowery lee,
Our gangrel cores met merrily
But now they're parted, sorrow speed them!
Amang some chiels that dinna need them –
Ilka slap and byeway's steekit,
Field to field is patched and eikit,
And naething's left for a puir body,
No a mouth's bite to a cuddy.
That auld guidmen wha graced the kinntrie,
Hae vanished a' in half a cent'ry;
Although their steadings shaw'd but meanly,
Their hearts were tender, warm and friendly;

They werna sae tae gear attached,
As chok'd their pity for the wretched;
Nor e'er sae puffed wi' fortune's feathers,
To make them spurn their luckless brithers –
Wi' rest and peace sure heaven has bless'd them,
But the poor hae sadly missed them.
Ye doughty dead, for you I'm grievin',
But I'll say naething o' the leevin';
To lack them I am ever mintin',
And to roose them would be sklentin';
Whate'er attendance fortune grants them,
The poor folks' blessing seldom haunts them:
Against our core throughout the nation,
There is an unco combination;
Ilk kintrie keeper's proudly struttin',
The constables hae been recruitin';
Tae catch ilk wight that bears a wallet,
Peace officers hae pawned their saul on't;
Tae chace the lazy, lame and crippled,
The border pack is now unkippled;
Loud rings the cry 'tween Kale and Ettrick,
To hunt each wanderer like a paitrick.

She said nae mair, for rising wrath,
  Tied up the carlin's tongue;
Wi' stalwart air, she held her breath,
  And shook a hazel rung.

THE CHARMS OF LIBERTY

What gives the bleakest region charms?
What is the nurse of arts and arms?
And every manly bosom warms –
   It is the smile of Liberty.

What makes science stretch her scan?
What doeth the flame of genius fan?
And rouses all that's great in man?
   It is the breath of Liberty.

But now this noble gift of Heaven,
Must from Europa's climes be driven;
For which her gallant sons have striven,
   And barter'd life for Liberty.

From her dark zenith slavery frowns,
Through her domains the war-note sounds,
And loudly calls on cowls and crowns
   To quench the light of Liberty.

 The doughty Bourbon's bared his sword;
Its point has often freedom gored;
And chill Siberia's savage horde
   Has vow'd the ban of Liberty.

As freedom stands their aim and thrust,
 And sees the storm of ruin burst,
She turns her eye where she was nurst,
   O'er to the isle of Liberty.

Britannia, belted with the wave,
Proud with the trophies of the brave,
Must either lend her hand to save,
   Or 'tend the bier of Liberty.

When she beholds devoted Spain
Fair freedom's sinking head sustain,
Her rampant lion shakes his mane,
   Roused by the shrieks of Liberty.

Oh! Spain's proud genius, burst your urn,
And bare the brand by freedom worn,
At Marathon and Bannockburn,
   These glorious fields of Liberty.

Pour Slav'ry, pour your swarms, but know,
Though countless, you're a feeble foe;
No energetic ardours glow,
   But in the cause of Liberty.

Let your cold vot'ries try to bind,
In bands of steel, the viewless mind;
And change the stamp of human kind,
   Ere they extinguish Liberty.

Make stately rivers landward glide;
Make winter walk in summer's pride;
And fix the ocean's restless tide,
   Ere they extinguish Liberty.

Let banded despots potent proud,
Becalm the stormy tempest loud,
And chain the bolt that cuts the cloud;
   And then extinguish Liberty!

WILL O' BOWMONT

Upon the bonny banks o' Bowmont,
   Thick wi' herds and hirsels spread,
In calm content for mony a towmont,
   A shepherd held a hamely shed.

He'd speel'd the brae o' live right wary,
   Where delusive phantoms glide;
But now he held his way right cheerie,
   Sloping down the sunless side.

He look'd on waning life wi' pleasure,
   He scarcely fand the tug o' time;
He had a son, his only treasure,
   Verging now on youthful prime.

Young Will, for manly shape and feature,
   Now stood peerless on the green;
His mind was richly wrought by nature;
   A' its movements quick and keen.

He melted at a mournful story,
   Indignant, swelled at stupid pride;
Sic minds are aye our nature's glory,
   While they stand on virtue's side.

But, ah! If vice perverts their current,
   They still retain their wonted force;
Reinless, like the mountain torrent,
   Dashing wild a headlong course.

A rumour raise about invading:
   Our lads sae loyal, true and staunch,
Flew to arms, and gaed parading,
   Busk'd in red to fear the French.

'Twas in this time o' din and riot,
   Will got warning on the hill,
To leave the haunts o' rural quiet,
   And tae gang and 'tend the drill.

When first he frae his glens was parted,
   Like other ill-bred country clowns,
He looked aghast and often started
   At the ways o' crowded towns.

But lured at last wi' flowing glasses,
   Will ran headlong into vice;
He soon forsook his barefit lasses,
   For some beauties no sae nice.

When his time drew to a finis,
   Will return'd withouten scars;
He'd learned indeed some tricks o' Venus,
   But little at the school of Mars.

Ilk rural joy had now grown tasteless,
   Still in his lug the music rung;
The lee lang day he listened, listless,
   To the lark or milkmaid's sang.

In regimentals busked, belted,
   Weekly to the town he ran;
He drank a hog or e'er he halted,
   And raise as dry as he began.

Sic ways wi' grief the rake remembers,
   As soon as he gets time to think;
Reflection fans up virtue's embers,
   Hafflins smoor'd, but not extinct.

To good advice Will never harked,
   But scatter'd a' the pickle gear;
He gaed ae day to see the market,
   Fell in, and drank the guid grey mare.

In sic ways he still persisted,
   His kin to stop him strove in vain;
Till ruin'd quite, at last he listed,
   And joined reinforcements bent for Spain.

TO A REDBREAST

Ye little crimson-breasted chield,
You've quickly left your haunts a-field,
   When angry skies are low'rin';
Hass Boreas, wi' a blust'rin' din,
Stripp'd a' the greenwoods to the skin,
   And left nae bields to cower in?

Though winter shows his hoary face,
Your comrades o' the feathered race
   Keep shyly at a distance;
While ye, the meanest o' the corps,
Come cringing to the cottage door,
   To seek for some assistance.

When simmer comes wi' mantel green,
You're then but seldom to be seen,
   Nae bird looks half so shyly;
Ye'll proudly hap from spray to spray,
Rejoicing in the warming ray,
   An' bear your head fu' highly.

 Like some whom fortune gie's a lift,
Aboon the level wi' her gift,
   Grows haughty, proud an' vain;
Grown giddy on a fancied height,
They e'e the toil-exhausted wight
   Wi' mighty great disdain.

The mind that tynes its equal poise,
Puffed up wi' fortune's glitt'ring toys,
   When adverse tempests blow,
Oft starts from its delusive dream,
An' strikes upon the next extreme,
   Both servile, mean an' low.

INSENSIBILITY AND SENSIBILITY COMPARED

The faded bracken browns the hill,
   No more the grove resounds wi' glee,
The day is brief, the breeze is chill,
   The leaf fa's quiverin' from the tree.

To see the summer from us part,
   And all her sweets bestrew the ground,
Cause the pensive, feeling heart
   Heave with a melancholy stound.

More blest his heart that ne'er beats high,
   In every shifting scene at ease,
Who looks with an unalter'd eye
   On bursting buds and leafless trees;

Whose bosom ne'er to rapture rose,
   That's ne'er depress'd nor e'er elate,
Whose tideless feelings scarcely knows
   To hope or fear, to love or hate;

That's ne'er misled by fancy's ray,
   Untroubled though his aim he miss.
When wandering in a thorny way,
   Insensibility is bliss.

Unwounded still, where wounds are rife,
   Rank'd on life's rough battlefield;
To save her sons in hottest strife,
   Kind dullness lends an ample shield.

Should fortune, with a kind regard,
   Look on such wi' indulgent eye,
They bask upon the flowery sward,
   Unmoved by misery's deepest sigh.

Though highest joys from feeling spring,
   Yet joys with man can ne'er remain;
Like quiver o' the lightning's wing –
   One flash and all is night again.

Like birds that feed upon flowerets fair
   Are minds that chase romantic bliss;
These feasts are few, such flowers are rare
   In such a wintry clime as this.

But if deep sorrow ever stound
   In hearts where ardent feelings play,
Though time may staunch the gushing wound,
   The scar it leaves remains for aye.

If fortune spread her glittering toys,
And all her sweets their path adorn,
In haste to grasp the flowering joys,
They often feel the rankling thorn.

As on life's stormy seas they sail,
No pilot rules till danger's past,
They, in the rudest, wildest gale,
With full-spread canvass, meet the blast.

If shivering poverty advance,
  They doubly feel the ills she brings,
They writhe beneath the scornful glance
  That haughty wealth at poortith flings.

And if in age they tread the glades
  Their youthful fancy deem'd so fair,
What meet they but departed shades
  Of love and friendship wandering there?

If those of happy, heedless mind,
  In age their youthful haunts review,
Perhaps no trace is left behind,
  But where the best potatoes grew!

But who would lose the pleasing dream,
  The feeling heart's high ecstacy,
Or give its momentary gleam
  For a whole age of apathy?

THE SONG OF THE PATRIOTIC ELECTOR

I'm an elector brave and bold, there's none presumes to
    doubt:
The struggling parties of the state, I give them vote about;
I soon forsook the Radicals, because their cash was low,
And that's enough to make me turn and dance Jim Crow.
  'Tis round about, and turn about, howe'er the wind may
     blow;
    With Tories, Whigs, or Radicals, I'm still Jim Crow!

I thought the Whigs would lift me up, to catch a gauger's
    name,
Or some snug berth, – but yet to me promotion never came.
They pledged and promised fair enough, but still per-
    form'd but slow –
I turn'd me to the Tories next, and danced Jim Crow!
    'Tis round about, Etc.

The Tory's creed being sage and short, I learn'd it in a
    crack –
To bless the Corn-laws and the Kirk, and curse O'Connell
    black.
Our wildest war-cry is the Church, and that's the note we
    blow
To make the Whigs start from the helm, and dance Jim
    Crow!
      'Tis round about, Etc.

But if the Tories can bestow nought on their friends but
    thanks,
Such pay will never make me dine, – I'll soon desert their
    ranks.
My heart is sick with hope delay'd, and I have told them so;
I'll turn me to the Whigs again and jump Jim Crow!
      'Tis round about Etc.

I'm none of those that are content with poverty and fame;
Like patriots in modern days I mind my house at hame.
Wealth brings us fame, and brings us friends, and whiles
    disarms a foe,
And often makes the ills of life to dance Jim Crow!
    'Tis round about Etc.

Chill poverty can blight the wreath that decks the bravest
    brow,
And partnership's been long dissolved 'tween rags and
    glory now,
Whate'er they were in days of yore, now wealth and
    worth's in Co.;
Let me get pelf, the Kirk and State shall dance Jim Crow!
    'Tis turn about Etc.

We are the life-blood of the Church, we're made a pious
    vow
To guard her glebes, lands, tithes and rates – this is reli-
    gion now.
The prelate and the presbyter their deadly feuds forego –
When pelf's at stake they join their hands and dance Jim
    Crow!
      'Tis round about Etc.

THE ENCHANTED CAVE

In days o' yore, when folks had often seen
Great bands o' fairies dancin' on the green;
When bogles wan beside ilk eldern thorn,
An' brownies coost their coats and thruish the corn:
'Twas in these days a shepherd watch'd his flocks,
In a deep glen, hung round wi' threat'ning rocks;
He in an instant saw the sky o'ercast,
An' heard the whistling o' a furious blast.
Deform'd wi' frowns, the brow o' nature lower'd;
The sounding rain in weighty torrents pour'd;
Quick through the gloom the nimble lightnings scud,
Their furious glances cleave the sullen cloud,
Broad sheets of flame wrap up the mountain's clift,
While loudly roars the artillery of the lift.
As down the rocky glen the tempest raves,
The echoes murmur in their hollow caves,
Down the steep peaks, where verdure never grew,
The streamlets trinkle o' a drumlie hue.

And still increasing made a deaf'ning din,
Wild dashing headlang, foam frae lin to lin.
The scene brought a' the deluge to his mind,
He thought the warld might get a second synd,
It made him blithe aneath some clints to cower,
To shun the pelting of the furious shower.
Far ben the rock he saw a glint o' light,
Then unco ferlies pass'd afore his sight;
A pond'rous door of iron open flew,
An' show'd three brimstone papers burning blue;
Within a cave wad held maist a' his flock,

Deep, lang an' wide roof'd o'er wi' solid rock;
Stretch'd on the pavement o' the cave was seen
Three men in armour o' a stalwart mein:
Their hounds, their hawks an' horses lay around,
An a' appear'd as they were sleepin' sound.
Far ben the cave he saw some odd-like things –
Strange fearfu' forms, tied firm tae brazen rings:
A monstrous horn right I' the entrance hang,
A sword within a scabbard large an' lang;
The sword he drew, but, judge his sad surprise,
When both the sportsmen rub their drowsy eyes!
He thrust the sword quick down its scabbard deep,
Then everything resumed its wonted sleep.
Near and more the hideous forms appear'd,
The piteous mane o' misery was heard.
An angry voice addressed him frae the eave,
The tone wi' dread might have appal'd the brave:

"O wretched coward! Had ye ne'er been born, –
Neither to draw the sword nor blaw the horn!
Had ye ta'en heart an' gien the horn a blaw,
Ye'd broke the spell, an' freed us ane an' a'!
For your neglect we wish ye ne'er to thrive, –
May ills pursue ye lang as you're alive;
May ghaists and bogles round your dwelling peep;
May fairies' midnight music scare your sheep;
May witchcraft charms o'er a' your gear prevail;
May brownies buff ye with their iron flail!"
His way out o' the cave he wrought right soon,
An' signed himsel' to a' the powers aboon.
The door was closed wi' a dreadfu' shock,
The sound was long re-echo'd frae the rock.
His bluid half frozen wi' the great surprise,
He often fell, but scarce took time to rise:
While doon the brae he row'd, an' while he ran,

Never sae frighted since he was a man;
He coost his vera shoon, an ran for fear,
For to win hame ere bogles were asteer.

Though polish'd nations boast o' reason's beams,
They strike alternate on the two extremes:
First credulous an' blind, they swallow a',
Then sceptics turn, a' nought believe ava.

EPISTLE
TO A FRIEND IN THE BEGINNING
OF THE YEAR 1826

Old time on his car, with unwearied brattle,
  Again has run round in his wonted career;
Except when he halted to gaze on a battle,
  He never has linger'd these five thousand year.

The years are like milestones behind him receding;
  The last one he pass'd he told twenty-five –
Blighting and blasting what mortals take pride in –
  The labours of age sink under his scythe.

As fades with the summer the flower of the valleys,
  As fades in the autumn the leaf on the trees,
Like the foam on the stream, or the gossamer palace
  That's wafted away with the wing of the breeze.

So fleets haughty man, with his darings and doings.
  Obscurity covers the monarch and clown,
Save some giant names that wrestle with ruin,
  Like Egypt's auld bouricks sae dour tae ding down.

Our age has some names, though we scan not their merits
  Napoleon who fought, and a Byron who sung, –
To wipe out the trace of these mighty spirits,
  Oblivion's besom may rub to the rung.

But many a name to forgetfulness fated,
  Whose memory scarcely survived their bier,
May still proudly rank where greatness is rated,
  By soothing a sorrow, or drying a tear.

But, ah, my rude muse! Thy poor pinion's too feeble
   To attempt the high strain of the moral and grave;
Thou'rt like the wee worm in the path of the eagle,
    Or the flow of a fountain to an ocean's wild wave.

In life's little day a thick dimness surrounds us;
   Of the past and the future we little can say.
Behind, before, a horizon dim bounds us, –
    'Tis safer to sing what we've seen in our day.

Grim war has his trump hung to wave on the willows,
   Since Gallia has got her lost Bourbon again,
And sea-girt Britannia sits queen on the billows,
    And Ferdinand's sovereign and tailor of Spain.★

There's one little spot that the turkey-cocks claw at,
   But that is a scuffle not worth our regard:
It's slipt me, but classic folks ken what they ca' it –
    It once was the land of the hero and bard.

The magnates of England are herding their pheasants;
   The Pope is recovering in part from his fa';
The Czar of Muscovy is graithing his peasants,
    To harry poor Poland whose back's to the wa'.

★Ferdinand gave a free pardon under his hand and seal to a number of the patriotic
nobles of Spain, but as soon as he found himself firmly seated on the throne, he brought
them to the scaffold. To atone for his perjury and murder, he spent much of his time in
sewing petticoats to the Virgin Mary.

So Europe requites the brave nation who saved her,
  When her shatter'd armies were flying in dread
From the merciless sword of the prophet, who braved her
  And threatened destruction to Christian and creed.

No more we are frightened by Radicals training;
  We never want loyalty till we wanted bread.
Trade has got such a lift by the genius of Canning,
  Our commerce extends to the graves of the dead.

At even, the peasant, though toil-worn and weary,
  With old musket arm'd, again leaves his shed,
And hies him away to the kirkyard so dreary,
  To guard those he loved in their dark, narrow bed.

Round those once lovely forms, in the darkness consuming,
  His fondness still lingers, as loath to depart.
Love and friendship are flowers in a wilderness blooming,
  Sweet natives of Eden still left in the heart.

But here I must stop, as my Pegasus stumbled
  Just when he was running his rapid career:
I am troubled to think the auld aver has tumbled
  Until I had wished you a happy new year.

I doubtna you're blythfu' that now I have halted;
  This while ye've been greeted till wishing's worn bare;
For you're of a class that's with compliments pelted,
  Whose prospects are blooming sae bonnie and fair,

And youth, health, and fortune before you are flaunting
  Fu' low to the latter the world will bow;
And, tent me, when all these allurements are wanting,
  She scowls like the Cheviot with clouds on his brow.

THE CONSTABLE'S RANT ★

We're the border watchmen;
Thieves may hide their head;
We'll keep a' in order
'Tween the Kale and Tweed.

We're a band o' brothers,
Pledge our noble corps;
We can wield a baton
Tightly in a splore.

The parson tries persuasion,
Moralists declaim,
Yet nothing but the baton
Thumps conviction hame.

Sentinels of justice,
Outposts of the law,
Our employment's noble,
Though our fees are sma'.

Honour waits on danger;
We often risk our lives,
When we march to capture
Tipsy tinklers' wives.

★These lines were written by way of ridicule of a staff of officials in the district, who, to a full conspicuousness of their authority, added an extra share of officiousness, which displayed itself in some ridiculous acts, in which even-handed justice could not be completely recognised.

Often when on duty,
We get desperate clanks
Frae those wandering gypsies,
Wi' their besom shanks.

If e'er the sons of riot
Should kick up a splore,
They shall taste our batons –
Drunkards we abhor.

And if they are not slacken'd
When their fob is toom –
If they lack a tippence,
Jeddart is their doom.

Although a single toothfu'
Ne'er can hurt the brain,
We've had scarce a mouthfu'
Fill the stoup again.

We're a band of brothers.
   Pledge our noble corps:
We can wield a baton
   Tightly in a splore!

THE WINTER'S DAY

The distant sun doth faintly peep
Out o'er the hills of Cheviot steep;
The slumb'ring landscape's covered deep,
  By winter's sway;
Stirr'd by ilk gust, the drifted heap
  Bedims the day.

No spot the glitt'ring scene beclouds,
Except the dusky distant woods;
Or darksome trace of wand'ring floods,
  Slow gurgling wide,
Whene'er the gath'ring shelvie shuds
  Do stem the tide.

The naked woods are bleak and lone,
With glitt'ring loads their branches groan, –
And all their tuneful inmates gone,
  No sounds we hear,
Except the tempest's hollow moan,
  Sae dull and drear.

The shiv'ring ploughman puffs his nieves,
No more his share the furrow cleaves;
The plough stands rusting in the wreaths,
  Adown the dale;
With constant toil the thresher heaves
  The sounding flail.

The nibbling flocks forsake the knowe,
And inward seek the shelter'd howe;
The sinking snaw they warsal through,
    In length'ning raws,
To where the broom and brambles grow
    In bieldy shaws.

The shepherd hastens to their aid,
With change of seasons undismay'd;
He flings about his bieldy plaid,
    Wi' manly mien;
Though winter scowls, in frowns array'd,
    He braves his spleen.

He mocks the silken sons of ease,
Who, placed around the ingl's bleeze,
And, lest their wee drap bluid should freeze,
    Oft toast their loof,
And start to hear the rustling breeze
    Rave round the roof.

The trembling maukin skips the heath,
Stung wi' a constant dread of death:
And, starting at her panting breath,
    She'll list'ning stand,
Her coward fears foreboding skaith
    From ilka hand

The ragged poacher speels the fell,
As easy scared as maukin's sel':
If prattling tongues his honour tell
    What he's about,
The law's train'd bloodhounds, fierce and fell,
    Wad find him out.

Ye poacher loons, I fear, I fear
This day will cost ye very dear;
When in the court it doth appear
  That Batie bled;
Stern justice growls like ony bear,
  And mercy's fled.

When the rude winds of winter roar'd,
'Tis vain to plead that hunger shoar'd
A helpless offspring round your board;
  Peace! ne'er begin –
Ye've marr'd the pastime of a lord –
  Ah! deadly sin.

In this loved land, where freedom reigns,
One only blot her mantle stains:
These old despotic feudal chains
  O' Gothic days,
That gall her healthy, hardy swains –
  Her pride and praise!

In danger's gloomy, darkest day,
They always prove their country's stay,
  On crimson'd field or flood;
Their breasts against a gaughty foe,
On the proud plains of Waterloo,
  A brazen bulwark stood.

Ye circles of the rich and gay,
Whose bowers defy the winter day,
  Where wealth and warmth abound;
Planted around the mantling bowl,
While mirth and music soothe the soul,
  And pleasure reigns around;

Amid your revels, call to mind
The hapless partners of your kind,
  Whom various ills distress,
In poor misfortune's hovels, low,
The bleak abodes of want and woe,
  And hopeless wretchedness.

THE SOGER AND THE SHEPHERD

SHEPHERD

Rest ye, rest ye, wounded soger,
　We hear there's been a bluidy fray;
You for this night shall be my lodger,
　And tell me wha has won the day.

Rumour frae her wings has shaken
　News that fill our hearts wi' pain;
We've heard our border band is taken,
　And its gallant chieftain slain.

SOGER

Our country still retains her honour,
　And will, I trust, while ages run:
Vict'ry sits upon our banner,
　But, alas!　it's dearly won.

We pass'd the border line undaunted,
　With the Douglas at our head;
When day declined our host encamped
　On the rugged banks of Reed.

The fading camp-fires faintly glanced,
　Our sogers press'd their grassy bed,
When the English host advanced
　By the daring Hotspur led.

The sleepless guard the camp alarm'd
  With the trumpet's rousing breath;
Our gallant sogers quickly arm'd,
  And form'd on the field of death.

Scotia's hammer high was rear'd,
  Studded o'er with trophies bright:
Her bloody lion grim appear'd,
  Muffled in the shades of night.

From each array, out quickly darted
  Rows of steely falchions bare,
And winged deaths from bowstrings started,
  Whizzing through the midnight air.

The fiery sparks, with nimble lightness,
  Round the temper'd edges play;
The battle's breast, in clust'ring brightness,
  Vied with the milky-way.

In deadly strife they long contended,
  Alternate shouts of success rung;
Vict'ry, high in air suspended,
  Long on doubtful pinions hung.

Douglas, danger's frown defying,
  Pierced the southron battle deep –
Raging like a chafed lion:
  Round him lay a lifeless heap.

Like to a bark, on rocks impell'd
  By the tempest's stormy breath.
His soul, by thirst of glory swell'd,
  Bore him on the points of death.

With spears and arrows deadly wounded,
  In the fierce and fatal fray,
With the wrecks of war surrounded,
  Bleeding, faint the hero lay.

A Scottish knight his fall espied,
  And quickly flew to his relief;
He seized his hand, in blood deep dyed,
  And hung in anguish o'er the chief.

"Knight," said Douglas, "cease your sighing;
  Tears let whining weakness shed;
Why do ye mourn a soldier lying
  Stretch'd on honour's lofty bed?

"With joy my lab'ring heart is lifting
  That I have 'scaped a coward's grave;
Now, when this mortal scene is shifting,
  I'll make my exit with the brave.

"The parted shades of mighty warriors,
  Who have this course of glory run,
From death's dark, dim, and gloomy barriers,
  Look exulting on their son.

"I know thou art to fear a stranger,
  O'er the field m banner call;
Proclaim that Douglas is in danger,
  But conceal your chieftain's fall.

"But why am I your ear engaging,
  Wasting time in useless words?
Still the doubtful battle's raging, –
  I hear the clang of deadly swords."

Where the conflict hottest raged,
　　Loud resounds the Douglas' name;
It cheer'd his hands, where'er engaged,
　　And fann'd their ardour into flame.

The Scottish spearmen, onward bearing,
　　Through the southron battle broke;
But Percy, still in danger daring,
　　Long withstood their dreadful shock:

This gallant chief, to fly disdaining,
　　Faint with wounds, and forced to yield,
Still his former fame retaining,
　　Won on many a bloody field.

The queen of night, her course pursuing,
　　Shed her pale and heatless beams,
And faintly mark'd the scene of ruin –
　　Mangled heaps and gory streams.

I view'd the field when horror lour'd,
　　And saw the lifeless Douglas lie;
The streams that from his bosom pour'd
　　Had drained all their fountains dry.

Of warriors brave, what goodly numbers
　　Saw the shades of evening close;
But cold and hush'd, in lasting slumbers,
　　When the morning sun arose.

The boasted pride of either border,
　　Wrapp'd in blood, and cold as clay,
Though lifeless, pale, yet ranged in order,
　　In their lines of battle lay.

LINES
SUGGESTED BY THE VISIT
OF THE CHOLERA

Our fathers, who were superstition's dull slaves,
Thought troubles were bounded like ocean's wild waves,
And only broke forth when a signal was given –
A signal on high from the Ruler of Heaven.

The fabric of nature our fathers ne'er scann'd,
Their dim spark of reason our fathers ne'er fann'd;
They met with diseases as judgments from God, –
All passive and humble, they bow'd to the rod.

Now reason, and science, and medical lore,
All tell us the days of weak whimsies are o'er;
Now tutor'd by science 'neath reason's bright ray,
We're manly and firm in calamity's day.

When cholera raged we lately were seen
To meet its approaches with dignified mien;
Whene'er we beheld the dread pestilence near,
Our life-guards were ordered to check its career.

They brandish'd their batons – how warlike the sight!
The sons of pale mis'ry fled back in a fright:
While we stood in safety behind their array,
Our gestures significant, seeming to say: –

"Now, death's sternest minister, dare you advance
'Gainst Crispin's stout cudgel and David's bright lance?
Beware of that lancet! its temper is good
At cleaving a cabbage and thirsting for blood.

"Beware of Crisp's cudgel, it was hewn by Nick,
And harden'd by Mammon, a merciless stick.
Whene'er it is brandish'd, woe, woe to the foe,
It captured a conq'ror at proud Waterloo.

"Ye two chosen champions, your name shall be given
To fame; let her blow till her trumpet be riven.
So great is your prowess, when guarded by you,
We need not the shield of omnipotence now."

But here let us pause – sure the muse is to blame;
How dares she to sport with so awful a theme?
A judgment so dreadful from Heaven's gone forth,
Appalling the nations that dwell on the earth.

It bursts unexpected, destroys, disappears,
Leaving thousands in dust and ten thousand in tears.
Its paths are in secret, its nature to scan
Defies all the boasted researches of man.

How woeful the day when the blight of its breath
Made Tweed's healthsome shores the arena of death!
Its aspect of terror relaxed natur's ties –
That bond of mankind which men's weakness supplies.

They seem'd as dissolving and falling at large,
For friends fled their friends, and some pastors their charge;
The dying were left to go down to the tomb,
Unaided by clergy, once infancy's doom.

Who values a shepherd that feigns a deep care,
In the hour of calm sunshine, when safety is there,
But shifts for himself in the hurricane's shock,
When the wild sweeping tempest is whelming his flock?

Who honours the chieftain who, in forays or war,
Acts only his part when all danger's afar,
But flies from the band when the battle comes on,
And leaves them to struggle and perish alone?

The poor pittanced soger to warfare goes forth
To bleed in the brawls of proud worms of th' earth;
Behold him on trial, from peril ne'er shrink,
But stand by his post on eternity's brink.

Can pastors to safety more dastardly cling?
They soldiers, yea leaders, for Sion's great King!
Their cause is the noblest, the warfare not hard,
The victory certain, and great their reward.

While rev'rend pretenders indignant we spurn,
With pleasure exulting, to Taylor we turn,
Who gain'd from his people loud plaudits of praise,
When tried by the touchstone of perilous days.

He watch'd for their weal when prosperity shone,
Nor did he forsake them when sorrows came on;
He taught them by precept where trust should be staid;
He taught, by example, the suff'rer to aid;

At the couch of the dying was earnest in prayer,
Suggesting the hopes that could banish despair;
Where doctors were wanting, for fees or for fame,
He dared to be seen in Messiah's great name;

Though death stalk'd around him, from duty ne'er swerv'd,
But left the event to the Sovereign he serv'd,
Urg'd by His example, who, whilst here below,
Ne'er yet kept aloof from the dwellings of woe.

Good Taylor's compeers his devotion have blamed –
They felt as did Cope when Gard'ner was named;
Yet deep veneration, for ages to come,
Will hallow his mem'ry when he's in the tomb.

His country applauds him, and hopes he will know
Far loftier plaudits than earth can bestow –
The approval of Heaven, upon that dread day,
When nature's dissolving, and time is away.

THE SHEPHERD'S ADDRESS
TO HIS AULD DOG

Hae, there's a morsel, honest fittie,
Ye're now grown auld, the mair's the pity;
I've seen ye frisksome, wild, and witty
        And brisk and gay;
Weel are ye worthy o' a ditty,
        The best I hae.

I've seem ye fit the benty fells,
Light as the lamb that skips the dells;
O' tods I have had twenty tails
        That ye had ta'en;
But what we've been it nought avails
        Yon days are gane.

Ten circling twalmonts ye hae seen,
And ever true and trusty been:
A faithfu' friend frae morn to e'en,
        'Mid care or strife;
And in some stormy nights, I ween,
        Ye saved my life.

Benighted in a lonely cleugh,
The dark'ning drift drave through the heugh;
The tempest howl'd wi' madd'ning sough,
        Wild o'er the waste;
It toil'd the hardiest frame enough,
        To brave the blast.

O'er many a moor and fen I crost,
Till every airt and aim was lost:
Benumb'd wi' bitter pincing frost
    Till nearly gane,
I gae to you're the leader's post –
    Ye brought me hame.

When fortune wi' an angry e'e,
Look'd sair askance and scowl'd on me;
The feck o' a' my friends but thee
    Forsook my side:
Scar'd we the ills I had to dree,
    Right sair to bide.

My doublet scarce wad hide my skin,
Cauld grew the looks o' a' my kin;
They pass'd my door, and ne'er came in,
    Forgat my name:
But on ilk day o' dool or din.
    Ye was the same.

Though scrimped o' your daily fare,
But little feck I had to spare,
Ye gat nae banes till they were bare,
    Sad tale to tell;
Sometimes the offals o' a hare
    Ye took yoursel'.

I've found in thee a faithfu' friend,
That sought to serve nae private end;
Ane that misfortunes ne'er could bend,
    Though o'er sae rife,
Ane wha his master to defend,
    Wad ventured life.

Although ye're feeble, fail'd, and auld,
And scarce do toddle to the fauld,
While I hae either house or hauld,
  Though o'er sae bare,
O' my last morsel, het or cauld,
   Ye'se hae a share.

SONG
THE BONNIE BANKS WHERE
TEVIOT STRAYS

Air: *"The Wood of Craigielee"*

Ye bonnie banks where Teviot strays,
   Ye bonnie banks where Teviot strays,
I lo'e thee still, though far awa,
   Seats o' my happy early days.

To cauld Canada's gloomy woods,
   Misfortune's train has hunted me;
I cheerless view those giant floods,
   And think them ill exchanged for thee.
     Ye bonnie banks, &c

Thy lovely landscapes deck my dreams,
   While fancy floats in reverie,
I wander by thy crystal streams,
   And nightly still revisit thee.
     Ye bonnie banks. &c.

When day succeeds the dreary night,
   And morning lifts his sparkling e'e,
I think his beams were twice as bright
   When glintin' o'er the Cheviot hie.
     Ye bonnie banks, &c.

The tuneless grove nae concert pours
   To greet approaching spring wi' glee;
And simmer spreads nae lovely flowers
   Like them I've often pu'd on thee.
     Ye bonnie banks, &c.

In every clime beneath the sun
   Fair friendship's ne'er a naked tree;
Some friends in distant lands I've won,
   But nane like those I left on thee.
      Ye bonnie banks, &c.

A dear and ardent wish remains,
   May fortune grant the boon to me –
In age to tread thy lovely plains,
   And spend life's gloamin' hour on thee.
      Ye bonnic banks, &c.

SCOTSMEN'S LOVE OF CREED
AND COUNTRY

Scotland's brother, stout John Bull,
Aye canty when his crib is full,
   Has sometimes jeer'd the Scot;
He says his sister suffers much,
So long as ye forbear to touch
     Her creed, or porritch-pot.

She wad be sweard her creed to tine, –
It cost her unco dear langsyne,
   Upon her hills and rocks;
Her creed commends her to be free,
But if it jarr'd with liberty,
    She'd think it hetrodox.

Langsyne her brose was sometimes thin,
She had nae time to plew nor spin,
   When foes were on her coast;
They on her bagpipes got a tune,
And after, when the reel was done,
    They had nae cause to boast.

TO A SWALLOW

Sporting in the genial beam,
Through the yielding air ye skim,
Out o'er the surface of the stream
    Wi' nimble wing:
Whiles to the banks where insects teem
    Ye twittering cling.

But, in a very little time,
You'll leave us for a warmer clime,
Where winter, wi' his cloak o' rime,
    Has ne'er been seen;
Where simmer wanders lang in prime
    'Mang woodlands green.

Where'er the beam of fortune warms,
Friends gather round in thick'ning swarms,
Fast plying flattery's nets and charms,
    And round us stand;
We're then receiv'd wi' open arms
    On every hand.

But, when the cloud begins to lour,
That bears misfortune stern an' sour,
They strive to shun with a' their power
    The coming blast;
Like insects chased before the shower,
    They scatter fast.

THE LAURELS OF SCOTLAND

1803

Still Europe is shaken with vengeful debate,
Both sides claim the vict'ry, but none the defeat;
But, if there's nae winning, let statesmen tell how
France came by these laurels she wears on her brow.

That Corsican callan surprises us a',
The sceptres o' Europe he's toss'd like a ba',
He's made kings an' kingdoms before him to bow,
An' laid a' their laurels on Gallia's brow.

At length, we are told, that he threatens sic things,
If once he had closed his creation of kings –
In spite of the ocean he will venture through,
To tear the auld laurel from Scotia's brow;

The gift o' her sons, who of old time forstood. –
The price o' this laurel was torrents of blood:
An' ever sin-syne, a' the broils she's come through,
For their sakes she has worn it wi' pride on her brow!

When Rome's haughty legions the world oppress'd,
Sought freedom themselves, to make slaves o' the rest;
Then their greedy eagles that never were fou',
Flew fierce at the laurel on Scotia's brow.

Our trumpets a constant alarum did ring,
An' wearied the eagles that were aye on the wing;
 They took to their ramparts to screen them, I trow,
Still leaving the laurel untouch'd on her brow.

An' many a battle for it she had fought,
Thro' fields clad wi' carnage for freedom she sought,
She made Bannockburn in red torrents to row,
In defence of the laurel she wore on her brow.

For losing her laurel still Scotland's not feared,
If her friends dinna sell it, her faes canna tear't;
An' still may she keep it while ages do row –
Still true independence encircle her brow!

FAREWELL TO CALEDONIA

Adieu, a lang an' last adieu,
   My native Caledonia;
For while your shores were in my view,
   I steadfast gazed upon ye, O!
Your shores sae lofty, steep, an' bold,
Fit emblem of your sons of old,
Whose valour, more than mines of gold,
   Has honour'd Caledonia.

I think how happy I could be,
   To live an' die upon ye, O!
Tho' distant many miles from thee,
   My heart still hovers o'er ye, O!
My fancy haunts your mountains steep,
Your forests fair, an' valleys deep,
Your plains, where rapid rivers sweep
   To gladden Caledonia.

Still mem'ry turns to where I spent
   Life's cheerfu' morn sae bonny, O!
Though by misfortune from it rent,
   It's dearer still than ony, O!
In vain I'm told our vessel hies
To fertile fields, an' kindly skies,
But still they want the charm that ties
   My heart to Caledonia.

My breast had early learn'd to glow
  At name of Caledonia;
Though torn an' toss'd wi' many a foe,
  She never bow'd to ony, O!
A land of heroes, famed an' brave,
A land our fathers bled to save,
Whom foreign foes could ne'er enslave!
  Adieu to Caledonia!

ADDRESS TO WAR

The muckle mischief ring ye're knell,
Infuried demon, nursed in hell;
Ye wi' your inventor fell
    Down deeps o' pain,
When he in Eden show'd himsel'
    Ye graced his train.

Thy black career began wi' time.
No tongue can tell in prose or rhyme
The waes ye've wrought in every clime;
    Thy deadly rage
Has swallow'd up creation's prime
    In every age.

What numbers on thy shrine ye've heap'd
What costly blood from it has dripp'd,
Its wi' the blood o' millions steep'd;
    Grim horrid sight!
Oh, had ye yon dark den but keep'd –
    Ne'er seen the light!

Besides the horrors of the plain
That groans beneath vast heaps o' slain,
A crowd of waes moves in your train,
    In mournfu' bands,
On every side the ruin'd swain
    Pale, shivering stands.

You've harrow'd Europe many years,
And still your horrid form appears:
Each land a dreary aspect wears,
  Where thou hast gone;
Though haflins drunk wi' orphans' tears,
  Ye stagger on.

Is there a wretch on either shore,
A demon dark creation's blore,
Who fans thy flame, or swells thy roar,
  While, snugly stow'd,
He grubs among his country's gore
  For witching gowd?

Oh, for that day, by seers sung,
When your rough trump shall lose its tongue –
Your car that oft o'er nations sprung
  Wild wasting wide,
Shall down the dark abyss be flung,
  There to abide!

THE WORM OF LINTON

In old days a monster, terrific and vast,
Had laid the green pastures of Teviotdale waste;
Its name, and its nature, and shape were its own,
It bore no resemblance to anything known;
Its head and its shoulders the crocodile claim'd,
The rest of its body a snake might be named;
It seem'd as if nature had veer'd from her plan,
And made all things hideous to centre in one:
The hugest of monsters that man ever saw
To it was a morsel scarce worthy its jaw!
On a smooth sloping upland, which rose near a fen,
In a torrent-scoop'd basin it had fixed its den:
For many roods round it the taint of its breath
Had scorch'd the green herbage, and blenched the heath.
All fearful of waging so hopeless a war.
Each living creature receded afar:
All eyes that beheld it recoiled at the sight.
The rook scream'd in terror, and quicken'd her flight.

When roused by hunger, destructive it roam'd.
And each thing it met with, it quickly intomb'd:
Rewards had been offer'd the monster to kill,
Yet still it had baffled all courage and skill.
Its back being fenced with a thick scaly shield.
Which mock'd all the weapons that mortals could wield.
When plied at a distance with arrows or darts,
And chanced to be gall'd on more sensitive parts,
The barb of the arrow scarce pierced the skin,
The wound of the dart seem'd a scratch of a pin;
No heart was so hardy to venture quite near,
To try in close combat the claymore or spear;
At sight of the monster even valour grew wan –
The task seem'd too vast for the prowess of man.

Alive to the luring of honour and fame,
Brave Elliot of Laristone enter'd his name;
His stern reckless valour was happy to find
Some desperate daring that daunted mankind!
The day of hard trial was publicly set,
A crowd from all quarters soon eagerly met,
Who, safe at a distance, stood silent and still,
And darken'd the summit of Wormington Hill:
Each striving of Elliot a glimpse to obtain,
Who, firm and undaunted, arrived on the plain:
He belted his broadsword, and mounted his grey,
To meet with a foe that held heroes at bay.
Not far from the den was a smooth, level mead,
Where nothing obstructed the tread of his steed:

To it he retired in firm, dauntless mood,
Where the monster pursued, grim, panting for blood.
His courser had borne him o'er many red fields,
'Midst blazing of broadswords and rattling of shields,
But soon as he saw the dread monster appear,
In spite of the spur he show'd symptoms of fear;
Its jaws wide extended display'd their dread forms,
Its eyes glared like meteors when muffled with storms,
Its growl was like sounds in a deep hollow cave,
Its throat seem'd a cavern as dark as the grave.
Thrice he eluded the grasp of this foe,
And found it unwieldy, its windings were slow;
Round it, and round it, he rode with swift bound,
And still, when he pass'd it, he gave a deep wound.
As the touch of the tempest arouseth the wave,
As the blast of the trumpet arouseth the brave,
As the breath of the furnace arouseth the flame,
As the spur stirs the courser till curbs cannot tame,

He found that his arm was too feeble to gore,
He only enraged it and chafed it the more;
No wound that he gave it could make it recoil,
His steed soon grew weary and wasted with toil;
He turn'd from the monster, unawed by its might,
But quickly returned in invincible plight:
Of hot burning turf he prepared a red roll,
Bound fast with green willows, and stuck on a pole;
When, with its vast jaws, to inclasp him it strove,
Down the throat of the monster the faggot he drove.

It writhed in anguish, and backward did start,
The smouldering fire soon scorched its heart:
The crowd at a distance, detained by fear,
With loud shouts of victory, exulting, drew near;
The echoes of Wormington caught the acclaim,
And tore the wide welkin with Laristone's name!

SONG

Air. – "Auld Langsyne"

To wander lang in foreign lands,
  It was my destinie;
I joyful was at my return,
  My native hills to see;
My step grew light, my heart grew fain,
  I thought my cares to tine,
Until I faud ilk weel-kenn'd spot
  Sae alter'd sin' langsyne.
    Auld langsyne, &c.

I sigh'd to see the flowery green
  Skaith'd by the ruthless pleugh;
Likewise the bank aboon the burn,
  Where broom and hawthorns grew:
A lonely tree, whose aged trunk
  The ivy did entwine,
Still mark'd the spot where youngsters met,
  In cheerful sports langsyne.
    Auld langsyne, &c.

I mixed with the village train,
  Yet still I seem'd alane;
Nae kindly hand did welcome me,
  For a' my friends were gane;
'Those friends, who oft in foreign lands
  Did haunt this heart o' mine,
And brought to mind the happy days
  I spent wi' them langsyne.
    Auld langsyne, &c.

In youthfu' prime, at fortune's ca',
   I braved the billow's roar;
I've now seen thirty simmer suns
   Blink on a distant shore;
And I have stood where honour call'd.
   In the embattled line,
And there left many gallant lads,
  The cronies o' langsyne.
         Auld langsyne, &c.

I've gather'd walth o' weel-won gear,
   Yet still I fortune blame:
I lang wi' strangers pass'd my days,
   And now I'm at hame:
I have nae friend, but what my gowd
   Can draw to mammon's shrine:
But how unlike the guileless hearts
  That wish'd me weel langsyne!
         Auld langsyne, &c.

NOTES

FASTEN E'EN – Page 12
"At the dumplings driving"

The dumplings here mentioned have from time immemorial formed and indispensable element in the rude festival of Fasten's E'en at Yetholm. The kickshaw, to be *au fait,* must be no brosey whip-together, but made of the finest flour, with currants to boot. Its origin, in connection with such an occasion is of very ancient date, and doubtless belongs to the era when the chime of minsterbells in the vales of Teviotdale spoke the high and palmy state of Romish power.

There are two matches at football played on Fasten E'en on the banks of the Bowmont, the one in Yetholm proper, the other in Kirk-Yetholm; and the mettle of old border character is seen in the ardour and agility with which the game is played. The gipsies, or muggers, whose great *howss* has for several generations been Kirk-Yetholm, turn out to warm their blood at a *bout,* and, from the desperate energy and hardihood which they display, they completely repudiate the stigma of indolence which their character as wayside *louts* all the year round obtains for them. Will Faa, who held the kingly honours of the tribe for many years, until he resigned them, towards the end of last year at the bidding of the King who makes the proudest crown to crumble, was one of the most celebrated football-players on the borders. For many years he bore the palm in all the great matches from beyond Millfield plain to far west of Yetholm. In his old age, when ninety-six years were on his head, his eye kindled with enthusiasm and his faltering tongue thrilled with eloquence as he recalled the feats and prowess of his youthful prime.

Cock-fighting, too, was another amusement at Fasten E'en, handed down from our jolly forefathers, and was most canonically observed up to late years. The schoolmaster, whether abroad or at home, favoured it with his especial patronage, so that the rising generation were never allowed to rust in the enjoyment of the practice. It formed a crack kind of sport therefore among the boys, and the shying at the heads of the defeated birds was a still more improving conclusion. Even church elders after the straitest fashion of Presbyterianism have been known to take delight in the bloody encounters of the Felton grey. The practice has, however, notwithstanding its vouchers of antiquity, has been entombed among the barbarities of the past, without scarcely finding a single apologist, as bullbaiting did in a famous statesman of his day, Windham.

———

THE WITCH'S CAIRN – Page 25

The author informs the editor that this piece was suggested on seeing a stone near to where he tended cows in his youth, which tradition pointed out as the spot where those horrible tragedies of witch-burning were perpetrated amid the pious maxims of our forefathers. There are several other places of a similar kind in the county: one at a place called Beggarmuir, on the estate of Hartrigge, near Jedburgh, belonging to Lord Campbell, where all offenders convicted of dark leaguing with powers of earth or air were dragged, to die a fiery death. The belief in witchcraft seems to have been one of the most terrible delusions that ever possessed any people. We read with sympathy and emotion the "book of martyrs" whom persecution has chased up to heaven; but we take no note or estimate of the number of poor unfortunate old women who must have perished in this and the neighbouring kingdom during the period that the awful delusion held sway. We shudder at the enormities of benighted Hindoos, yet what a state of things does orthodox Scotland present even up to the beginning of the last century! The last death of the kind at Beggarmuir is supposed to have taken place in 1696, the victim being a woman of the name of Shortreed, belonging to Jedburgh. So late as 1722, the sheriff-substitute of Sutherland consigned a poor wretch to death for some offence, under the act against witchcraft. This is said to have been the last case of the kind in Britain – the last *judicial* conviction, for we find, in White's "Natural History of Selborne," a case mentioned where some mad-headed peasants in Hertfordshire, in 1762, flung two old women into a well, on a charge of witchcraft ! In good sooth, the less that is said the better about the wisdom of our ancestors, as a maxim of authority!

THE CHEVIOT GAMES – Page 35

These games have been held from time immemorial at Pennymuir, an old hostel on Kale water. They consist of leaping, wrestling, and the other athletic exercises for which the Borders have long been famous. We occasionally see in illustrated London journals, about the periods of royal visits, pictorial representations of these games as they are held in the Highlands; but it is a fact that the feats there exhibited are quite poor. Donald, with all the rugged energy for which he is famous, has never been a great *athlete.* Professor Wilson, in an article in "Blackwood's Magazine," has said that a Border farmer has been known beat all the Highlanders that ever encountered him in these exercises, to sticks; and time was when old Kit himself could have taken the shine out of the best Highlander that ever stepped. And we would like to hear of anyone of the mountain who could come within a couple of yards of William Leyden of Denholm's tremendous performance of sixteen yards at a running hop, step, and leap. The Cheviot Games are, however, not altogether without exception on moral grounds in their consequences, like most rude sports of the kind, and "broken shins and noses" are often got and given before the sport is ended.

EPITAPH ON ADAM DAVIDSON – Page 60

Something more than a mere allusion is due to the memory of this very singular man. He spent the latter part of his life in Morebattle, and died there about twenty years back. At one period of his life he taught a school in Bonjedward, near Jedburgh, and his pupils still remember him as a man of a stern, unbending character. The people in those times seem to have been contented with no great acquirements in the instructor, as Davidson's scholarship was of a slender sort. He seems to have possessed a fund of strong common sense and quiet irony, which, being always exercised in the assertion of just principles, obtained for him an amount of deference not often rendered by villagers to their equals in station. His love of justice was a prominent feature in his nature. All tyranny and violation of fair dealing, no matter from whom, drew down his fearless denunciation. That feeling was not confined to mere words, for he would carry his cause and dispute the claims of over-reaching avarice or injustice before the local courts. He had the strongest desire to see his neighbours so far practise honesty and justice as not to offend one another by a disregard of social duties. As the arbiter of disputes of all kinds, he was regarded with the most implicit confidence. The consistent profession of these qualities consequently invested him with the highest respect n the eyes of the population. The author of the "Elegy in a Country Churchyard" must have had some such character in his eye when he remembered

> "the village Hampden, that with dauntless breast
> the little tyrant of his fields withstood."

A dispute once occurred in Morebattle between the feuars and the factor of the lands on which the village is built, regarding the removal of some trees which encumbered the little gardens – and act which the functionary mentioned refused to permit. Davidson was possessed, however, of legal acuteness, and determined to grapple with their antagonist. He held that the factor's opposition was unjust and illegal, and immediately braved the consequences by hewing down the obnoxious trees in defiance of the threats of prosecution. It turned out, however, that the weaver was right, as the other party forbore all proceeding in the matter. The rest of

186

the villagers, therefore, emboldened by the example set them, fell to work and made the clearance they desired.

During the trying period of the dear years, at the commencement of the present century, in order to commend economy in the use of the means of subsistence, the gentlemen of the county, headed by the then Duke of Roxburghe, issued a series of hints or instructions addressed to the public, among which was set forth the unthriftiness of people using bread too recently baked. This tickled our village Timon much; and after venting his satire on the great ones of the country investing a maxim known and practised by every cottar's wife in the country, with official importance, he addressed himself on the subject to the Duke of Roxburghe in a letter, in which he is said to have told some plain down truths. But a circumstance that obtains for him the most cherished remembrance was his publishing a reply to the Rev. Alexander Shanks of the Associate Congregation, Jedburgh, who had preached and published certain discourses, entitled "Peace and Order." This was in the year 1794, and was intended by the respected preacher, doubtless with the best of motives, to assist in allaying the feeling of discontent existing in this country in consequence of the progress of events in France. Davidson, obscure and poor as he was, and labouring under difficulties unknown at the present day, with its facilities of printing &c., regarded the views of the reverend gentleman as inculcating the divine right of things as they are after a too servile fashion, and appeared in print to break a lance with his more famed antagonist. The production was circulated and read with avidity, and obtained great fame for its author by its force and cleverness. Its effect was, however, much neutralised by the unfortunately but too successful efforts which were made by the authorities to purchase it up, who felt alarmed at the enthusiasm with which it was received as a defence of the more popular side of a public question. He likewise appeared in public as the author of a pamphlet entitled "The Sin of Encroachment," in which the rapacity that has swallowed up so many of our commons and rights of way received a forcible exposure.

Davidson's views of religious association were, in the eyes of the people of that age, peculiar; and he followed them out, fearless of that oral proscription which, in rural districts, not unfrequently overtakes any one who leaves the beaten path of use and wont. He held no connection with any of the religious bodies of the village, but on Sabbath kept retired in the privacy of his own fireside altar. He possessed a good selection of the more eminent and learned divines, and in conning and meditating over their pages he spent his Sabbaths.

His death, as we have said, took place about twenty years ago, but a remembrance of him is still gratefully cherished. In a publication like this, whose interest is in a large degree of a local nature, the Editor hopes these few remarks on a character not often presented "in our village" are not out of place. It is curious to find a remembrance of him surviving to this day. Although he gained no honour such as the "Montyan prizes," still he has found an admirer, yet no relation, to tender a word of melodious praise in the epitaph printed in the foregoing poems. It would be curious in an age like the present, when the philosophy which studies the influences on mankind, flowing out of the operation of the active single minds, is popular, to speculate on the way in which that humble individual may have affected his fellow-men.

As we have mentioned Mr Shanks's name, we ought to do him full justice in quoting the circumstance of the publication of the discourses. They were regarded so highly as to attract the notice of George the Third and his Government, and a communication through the Home Secretary was received by Mr Shanks, conveying a desire on the part of his Majesty to bestow some preferment or mark of favour on him. The sturdy preacher, however, returned for answer that he declined all reward for doing what he thought his duty, and that he belonged to a church in which there was neither preferment nor promotion, and the only promotion he desired was promotion in grace, in order to be a more efficient professor of his office.

—∽∿∼—

ON THE FALLING DOWN OF HOWNAM KIRK BELL – Page 84

This event, so pleasantly and somewhat oddly chronicled in the poem, occurred about half a century ago, and is well remembered to this day from the important circumstances connected with it. As is known to all connoisseurs in the operation of uncanny spirits, the kirk bell, from its religious association, had the power of keeping at a distance the powers of earth or air. Probably the fact that in some Roman Catholic countries of the people ringing the church bell during thunder storms, and the use of the dead or passing bell in olden times, by tolling it and the placing it at the foot of the corpse, may both have originated in the same feeling of faith in the potency of the agent. The falling of Hownam bell was soon felt as a most luckless calamity, it being attended with the most remarkable rush of "black spirits and white", and of all the other hues, into the district, to the very terror and annoyance of the lieges. The state of matters became intolerable, and it was found necessary, after the most serious injuries had been received by the decent rustics from the cantrips of the visitants, to restore the bell to its wonted position, which soon secured the quietness and order formerly enjoyed.

THE ORDINATION – Page 88

Morebattle seems to have been the scene of several violent settlements consequent on the enactment of the act of Queen Anne. The events as narrated in the poem occurred in the ordination of a Mr Christie. They are given much in the same way as the traditions of the district have been handed down; and it would appear that no little warm blood had been shown on the occasion by both sides. The hero styled Nub, who figured so valiantly, was so called from having a nub or club foot. He generally went by the name of Nub of Bowmont; and although lame in one sense, he was not so in another, as he united great physical strength with daring qualities of mind and character, with not a little of the Burley in his stern Presbyterian devotion. It is told that he came over the hills from Bowmont on the morning of the occasion, heading a party of friends, all armed with clubs, and eager for the fray. They gained entrance into the church by melting the lead that held the window iron stauncheons, and these they appropriated for "the battaille stour". The presentee, as narrated in the rude epic, turned out another man than the parishioners had anticipated, and a highly consistent and Christian deportment in the course of years caused the asperities of his settlement to be forgotten. Even Nub, so the story goes, extended the hand of friendship in the end.

It would be unfaithful, in recording a few of the local incidents connected with this volume, to forget the celebrated event of Gateshaw Brae, in the shape of a disruption from the Established Church, and to the formulation of a congregation in connection with the infant Association Synod, in 1739, and the celebration of the same event by centenary services in 1839. The 17th day of October in that year was one of the loveliest that ever shone. The beautiful green hills that run with wavy outline out from the Kale towards Primside were tinted with the withering fern that told of the waning year. The sun came in his strength, and from a cloudless blue made everything to glow with the mellow lustre of autumn. The day seemed the very "bridal of the earth and sky". Everything was in unison with the occasion that was to draw several thousands of human beings from their wide-scattered homes to do homage to the sacred principles that had excited the deepest interest of their forefathers a hundred years before. Gateshaw Brae was hallowed in the remembrance of the district as the scene of the meetings of the Covenanters when the brands of Claverhouse and his madmen flashed persecution. On this day were assembled three thousand people, forming one of the most interesting spectacles ever witnessed in that part of the country. Discourses and devotional exercises were sustained by various dissenting ministers from the neighbouring towns and villages. Nothing could be finer than when from the vast multitude there arose "the song, the loud acclaim of praise", with a volume and majesty worthy of an occasion which had taken for itself that

> "Temple, not one made with hands,
> The vaulted firmament."

It seemed "to take the soul of that waste place with joy." Emotions of no every-day character fill the mind in participating in an event which recurs only with the interval of one hundred years. Before the sacred centenary can again be celebrated, almost every human being who mingled in the crowd of Gateshaw Brae on that day will have mixed with his kindred dust. It was, in truth, an occasion on which, whatever grateful feelings might fill the mind, might well recall the pensive utterance of the leader of the Persian host as they arrayed themselves previous to setting out on their expedition against Greece.

As the early ripe sun glints of that October afternoon fell on the Cheviots, the irregular streams of human beings spreading themselves in all directions along the footways and hillsides indicated by the conclusion of an occasion that can never be forgotten by a single individual who had the privilege of being present.

—⁓—

TO THE SHADE OF WALLACE – Page 106

There is a reference made in this poem to the late Earl of Buchan, who erected a giant statue as an offering to the memory of the illustrious chief. It stands on a commanding eminence, overlooking the Vale of Tweed, near Dryburgh, and is really a very striking object. Although possessing a rough outline, it reflects no little honour on the artist, Mr Smith of Darnick. The fierce and warlike features of the Knight of Elderslie are most faithfully presented, so far as a likeness to the portrait in some of our old historical works enables us to judge. In front of the statue is an urn, on which are inscribed a few lines by an obscure poet of this district whose fate has been oblivion. His name was George Noble. From accounts and fragments of pieces that have survived of him, he appears to have been a man of considerable talent, though occupying no higher station than that of a day-labourer. In addition to being a votary of the muse, he was an adept in astronomical knowledge. His appearances as a poet were mostly confined to the publication of short pieces in the local papers. A regular publication of his poems was intended to have been carried out, in order that, with the proceeds, a tombstone might have been erected to his memory, but the scheme was stopped. He was born at Kersfield, a place on the north-west base of the Dunion Hill, but now entirely swept away. Hard work and fatigue affected his health, unfitting him to follow his usual occupation as a labourer, when the Earl of Buchan procured him a situation as a clerk in a colliery in Gateshead, where he remained until his death in 1816.

THE GYPSY'S RANT – Page 129

It would be supererogatory in a work of this nature to enter into any lengthy statements regarding the Gypsy tribe. A full description of this class of people and their local connection is given in Jeffrey's "History of Roxburghshire." We may mention one circumstance which is not contained in that work, viz., their location and original settlement in Yetholm, which village, as is well known, has been their great rallying point for several generations. The account which we have heard from the lips of one conversant with the traditions of the district is as follows:- When the Rebellion of 1715 was taking place, a portion of the insurgent forces passed through the district, and of course were not very scrupulous is drawing distinctions between *meum* and *tuum*. One of the rebels carried a very fine blood horse from the adjoining estate of Marlefield, belonging to and occupied by Sir William Bennet, a friend of Thomson the poet. The baronet, enraged at his loss, employed a stray gypsy who was lingering in the neighbourhood to recover the animal, in which he succeeded by following the troops and cutting away the fastenings of the horse in the encampment, under cover of night. Sir William rewarded the gypsy by giving him a house in Kirk- Yetholm to live in, and in that village they have preserved a footing to the present day. They possess a right of pasturage on the common, and rank as equals with the other inhabitants in all rights of the place.

ON THE VISIT OF THE CHOLERA – Page 161

This poem refers to the period when several of the Border towns shared in the visitation of cholera about sixteen years ago. The Mr Taylor alluded to was then the minister of the Relief Church, Coldstream, now the respected minister of the United Presbyterian Church, Hutchison Street, Glasgow. He pursued his ministrations to the sick and dying with fearless exposure during the height of cholera in Coldstream, which exertions did not fail to bring down on him some mean detraction, as well as the approving testimony of grateful fame for his noble conduct.

—◦◦◦—

THE WORM OF LINTON – Page 178

Opposite to Morebattle, on the other side of the Kale, is Linton, celebrated for its tradition of the worm, or serpent monster, which enjoyed a most terrible reputation for many centuries. Tradition has invested it with qualities which make it as difficult a subject for more sober fact to identify, as its equally celebrated congener the sea-serpent has ever been to the naturalist. Its den is said to have been in a recess to the east of Linton Hill, whence it prowled about, spreading blight and devastation wherever it went. Rewards were freely offered to any who would destroy it, but in vain, until a hardy wight essayed the perilous adventure, and, to the great relief of the country, after a temporary defeat, accomplished the destruction of the monster, by plunging a red-hot peat down its throat. Extensive lands in the parish of Linton were his reward. The names of Elliott and Sommerville have each laid claim to the traditionary honour, but we believe it is generally assigned to the latter family, who retain a recognition of it in their heraldic bearings. To what original germ of incident such a mythic story as this is to be imputed, is only a subject for speculation. Many districts in various countries seem to have a legend resembling it, in which a champion Hercules gained honour by signal services in assisting his fellows to subdue the savageness of unreclaimed nature. Our own John Leyden, one of the most gift-ed men whom Roxburghshire has produced, has remembered the legend in his patriotic poem of the "Scenes of Infancy," and has given it a more poetical rendering:

> "Pure blows the summer breeze o'er moor and dell
> Since first in Wormswood the serpent fell;
> From years in distance lost his breath he drew,
> And with the ancient oaks the monster grew,
> Till venom, nursed in every stagnant vein,
> Shed o'er his scaly sides a yellow stain;
> Save where upreared, his purpled crest was seen
> Bedropt with purple drops and streaks of green.
> Deep in a sedgy fen, conceal'd from day,
> Long ripening on his oozy bed he lay,
> Till, as the poison-breath around him blew,
> From every bow the shrivell'd leaflet flew,
> Grew moss began the wrinkled trees to climb,
> And the tall oaks grew old before their time.
> On his dark bed the grovelling monster long
> Blew the shrill hiss and launch'd the serpent prong,
> Or, writhed in frightful coils, with powerful breath,
> Drew the faint herds to glut the den of death –
> Dragg'd with unwilling speed across the plain
> The snorting steed, that gazed with stiffen'd mane –
> The forest bull, that lash'd, with hideous roar,
> His sides, indignant, and the ground uptore.
> Bold as the chief who, 'mid Lerna's brake,
> With mighty prowess quell'd the monster snake,
> To rouse the monster from his noisome den,
> A dauntless hero pierced the blasted fen.
> He mounts, he spurs his steed; in bold career,
> His arm gigantic wields a fiery spear;
> With aromatic moss the shaft was wreathed,
> And favouring gales around the champion breathed;
> By power invisible the courser drawn,
> Now quick, and quicker, bounds across the lawn;

194

Onward he moves, unable now to pause,
And fearless meditates the monster's jaws –
Impels the struggling steed, that strives to shun,
Full on his wide, unfolding fangs to run;
Down his black throat he thrusts the fiery dart,
And hears the frightful hiss that rends his heart;
Then, wheeling light, reverts his swift career.
The writhing serpent grinds the ashen spear, –
Roll'd on his head, – his awful, volumed train
He strains in tortured folds, and bursts in twain.
On Cala's banks his monstrous fangs appal
The rustics pond'ring on the sacred wall,
Who hears the tale the solemn rites between,
On summer Sabbath, on the churchyard green."

The present church of Linton – a curiosity in many respects – contains in its southern wall a piece of rude sculpture representing the valorous deeds of the "wud laird of Lauriston," as the conqueror was called. The production is about as quaint an affair as ever came from the land of Phidias. Situated where it is, however, it bears a kind of *ex cathedra* testimony in favour of the legend. The half-decayed figure of a man, with a falcon perched behind him, is seen attacking with a long spear something approaching to the common representation of a dragon. The sculpture doubtless belongs to a date long antecedent to the erection of the church, into which it must have been transferred from some other quarter.

The mound or hillock on which the present church of Linton stands is the subject of a curious tradition. It is said to have been formed by two maiden sisters as penance for some mortal crime committed by a brother, and to have been entirely thrown up with riddled sand. But the story is too familiar all over the country to be detailed here.

ADDENDA

Most of the poems which Davidson published in his earlier volume of 1825 also appear in *Leaves*. The few earlier poems which do not appear in *Leaves* now follow. Note that the second half of the first poem *Elliot of Laristone* appears earlier in this collection as *The Worm of Linton*.

ELLIOT OF LARISTONE

Bright blazed the taper in Laristone ha',
The bagpipes did boom, and the bugles did blaw,
The banquet was spread by the hand of the fair,
Stout yeomen, and bowmen, and spearmen were there;
Carousing, rejoicing, so bravely had sped
The foray, by Elliot of Laristone led:
Through the tower's lofty arches the martial airs rung,
The porches with corslets and helmets were hung,
The claymores in scabbards awhile did recline,
While warriors sought solace in beauty and wine.
Up rose an old minstrel, with locks like the snow,
His eyes shot mild lustre like suns wearing low;
As soon as his lyre he sounded with grace,
The wild and romantic arose in his face –
The eyes of the warriors were turn'd on the bard,
His theme was battles where dangers they'd shared;
He sang their last foray in heart-stirring strains,
Recounting their daring, their glory and gains;
He gave to each hero his chaplet of fame,
And fix'd a bright wreath on brave Laristone's name.
- He alter'd his lyre to wailings of woe;
He sung of brave comrades by foemen laid low;
His deep plaintive numbers soon moisten'd each eye,
And quenched the beams that in battle burnt high:
They praised, applauded, and pledged him in wine,
He then turned his harp to a lay of langsyne:
Cent'ries and seasons have fled on swift wing,
Since the days of the hero whose daring I sing;
Yet still he stands high in the legends of fame,
No long lapse of ages can moulder his name.

THE SONG

Laristone's chieftain the foray had join'd,
Where all the moss-troopers their powers had combined –
With true-hearted lads, o'er the border did hie,
To plenish their mailens with Cumberland kye.
They marched in silence o'er moss and o'er moor,
The night it was dark and the southron secure;
They seized a herd, and drove on till the dawn,
They were not expecting a sword to be drawn;
But Lowther got warning and muster'd his men,
And placed them in ambush down in a low glen –
The Scots were surprised, when pursuing their course,
With the bugle's shrill note, and the hoof-clang of horse –
Unsheath'd were the claymores that often had shone,
The warriors were halted, the booty drove on:
Bold Lowther enraged, rush'd wild on the Scot,
Both parties were brave, and the conflict was hot,
Until the moss-troopers their object had gain'd,
The booty away, and the foemen detain'd;
They then thought no longer of tempting the day,
They wheel'd from the battle and follow'd the prey,
– To Elliot of Laristone, booty seem'd light,
Being greedy of glory, continued the fight,
Though his yeomen were few, they were vet'ran and brave,
They bore each assault as the rock doth the wave;
On front, flank, and rear, when they did enclose,
They formed a death-ring and fronted their foes.
Fresh succours to Lowther incessantly pour'd,
And still they were sinking 'neath Laristone's sword –
So struggles the lion when caught in the toils,
Appall'd by his prowess the bravest recoils;
So great were the odds that his valour was vain,
O'erpower'd by numbers, his yeomen were slain:
Himself faint and sinking 'neath many a wound,

Was taken by foemen and ruthlessly bound.
Stern Lowther, enraged, no mercy would show,
His pastures were plunder'd, his bravest laid low;
He doom'd the young hero in irons to lie,
In the gloom of a dungeon, with hunger to die.
Lowther's fair daughter to meet him came forth,
The boast of the border for beauty and worth;
She gazed on the captives with pity and awe,
But turn'd pale as death when she Laristone saw:
In him she remembered the hero again,
Who freed her from miscreants who murder'd her train;
His sword, quick as lightening, decided the strife,
And saved Annie's liberty, honour and life!
Since that hapless day she had never found rest,
The youth that rescued her still haunted her breast;
His name or his country she never could know –
Nor deemed it was Elliot, her father's chief foe!
She'd seen his fine features, in danger grow keen,
She saw him in ruin, now calm and serene;
On that very day she was saved by his sword,
She ardently loved him, but now she adored –
She sued for his pardon, but all was in vain,
No pardon for Laristone she could obtain!
On that very day he was brought to his doom,
And laid in a dungeon design'd for his tomb,
The vassals of Lowther around did combine,
The night was devoted to revels and wine;
All but young Annie seemed joyful and gay,
Her heart in the dungeon with Laristone lay!
When all her stern kindred were draining the bowl,
The key of his prison at midnight she stole;
Though fearful and bashful, yet love made her bold,
She plied her servants with handfuls of gold;
They to their young lady soon swore to be true,
Then straight from the dungeon they Laristone drew.
The first time he saw her, he loved the fair dame,

Now, fanned by gratitude, blazed his flame –
"Forgive me, fair Annie, I cannot be free,
"Except you go with me my partner to be:
"The rage of your sire, all bounds will defy,
For saving a foe he has doomed to die –
"I'm not so unworthy of honour and thee,
"To leave you behind here, a victim for me;
"No death seems so dreadful, no dungeon so drear,
"To me, as the ruin of one I hold dear."
– So argued the chieftain the lady to move,
All reasons are potent when moved by love –
At length she consented with Elliot to go,
And share in his fortunes, come weel or come woe;
She beckon'd a servant – the steeds were brought forth,
And soon these two lovers set out for the north.
– To baulk all pursuers lone bye-ways they beat,
The moon shone unclouded, the coursers were fleet,
They rudely were stopp'd near the dawn of the day,
By seven rank reivers a-prowling for prey:
Three of them fell lifeless 'neath Laristone's hand,
The others receded in dread of his brand.
Appalled to see how their boldest had sped,
They poured their arrows, and dastardly fled;
But from them came whizzing, an ill-fated dart,
Which smote Annie's bosom, and pierced her heart!
The last leaden chillness shot swiftly through her frame,
She turn'd to her lover and faulter'd his name –
The chieftain grew frantic, and wild at the deed,
He caught her when sinking down faint from her steed!
Dim was her eye and her check pale as clay,
The rose's bright tinges were vanish'd for aye;
The cold hand of death soon extinguish'd her charms,
She heaved her last sigh in brave Laristone's arms.
Sore shook the chieftain, – the hero was fled –
High heaved his bosom and inwardly bled;
His face it grew wan as a statue of woe,

And wet was the eye that gleam'd fierce on a foe.
He sent for his servants and bore her away,
He laid her fair dust where his ancestors lay;
So sharp was his sorrow, so lasting its trace,
No smile ever after was seen in his face;
His mind was of peace and serenity reft,
Yet mid the convuision his valour was left:
When war scowl'd around him, he sought for repose
In the tumult of battle, more still than his woes –
The arm of the wretched is dreadful in strife,
So heedless of danger, so reckless of life.
– In those days a monster, terrific and vast,
Had laid the green pastures of Teviotdale waste;
Its name, and its nature, and shape were its own,
It bore no true semblance to any thing known;
Its head and its shoulders the crocodile claimed,
The rest of its body as snake might be named;
It seemed as if nature had veer'd from her plan,
And made all things hideous to centre in one:
The hugest of monsters that man ever saw,
To it was a morsel scarce worth its jaw!
On a smooth sloping upland which rose near a fen,
In a torrent scoop'd bason it had fixed its den –
For many roods round it the tint of its breath,
Had scorche'd the green herbage, and blenched the heath.
All fearful of waging so hopeless a war,
Each living creature receded afar;
All eyes that beheld it recoil'd at the sight,
The rook scream'd in terror and quicken'd her flight, –
When roused by hunger, destructive it roam'd,
And each thing it met with, it quickly intomb'd:
Rewards had been offer'd the monster to kill,
Yet still it had baffled all courage and skill,
Its back being fenced with a thick scaly shield,
Which mock'd all the weapons that mortals could wield.
When plied at a distance with arrows or darts,

And chanced to be gall'd on more sensitive parts,
The barb of the arrow scarce pierced the skin,
The wound of the dart seem'd a scratch of a pin;
No heart was so hardy to venture quite near,
To try in close combat the claymore or spear, –
At sight of the monster even valour grew wan,
The task seem'd too vast for the prowess of man.
- Alive to the luring of honour and fame,
Brave Elliot of Laristone enter'd his name;
His stern reckless valour was happy to find
Some desperate daring that daunted mankind!
The day of hard trial was publicly set,
A crowd from all quarters soon eagerly met,
Who, safe at a distance, stood silent and still,
And darken'd the summit of Wormington Hill;
Each striving of Elliot a glimpse to obtain,
Who firm and undaunted arrived on the plain:
He belted his broad sword, and mounted his grey,
To meet with a foe that held heroes at bay.
- Not far from the den was a smooth level mead,
Where nothing obstructed the tread of his steed; –
To it he retired in firm dauntless mood,
The monster pursued, grim, panting for blood. –
His courser had borne him oe'r many red fields,
Midst blazing of broad swords and rattling of shields,
But soon as he saw the dread monster appear,
In spite of the spur he show'd symptoms of fear;
Its jaws wide extended display'd their dread forms,
It eyes glared like meteors when muffled with storms,
Its growl was like sounds in a deep hollow cave,
Its throat seem'd a cavern as dark as the grave:
Thrice he eluded the grasp of this foe,
And found it unwieldy, its windings were slow; –
Round it, and round it, he rode with swift bound,
And still, when he pass'd it he gave a deep wound.
- As the blast of the trumpet arouseth the brave,

As the breath of the furnace arouseth the flame,
 As the spur stirs the courser till curbs cannot tame,
He found that his arm was to feeble to gore,
He only enraged it and chafed it the more;
No wound that he gave it could make it recoil,
His steed soon grew wary, and wasted with toil;
He turn'd from the monster, unawed by its might,
But quickly return'd in invincible plight, –
Of hot burning turf he prepared a red roll,
Bound fast with green willows and stuck on a pole;
When, with its vast jaws, to inclasp him it strove,
Down the throat of the monster the faggot he drove;
It wreathed in anguish, and backward did start,
The smouldering fire soon scorched its heart; –
The crowd at a distance detained by fear,
With loud shouts of victory, exulting drew near;
The echoes of Wormington caught the acclaim,
And tore the wide welkin with Laristone's name!

THE FATE OF EDWIN

The dull and dreary mirky night
  Trode on the skirts of twilight gray;
Nought but the Cheviot's distant height
Retain'd the tinge of parting day;

When Edwin and his hapless train,
  Try'd oft a lodging for to win;
At many a door they call'd in vain,
For none would let the wretched in.

His helpless offspring by his side,
  For them his tortured bosom bleeds;
Nae shelter but the welkin wide,
This night to screen their harmless heads.

His mem'ry muster'd happier days –
  Hard was the fate he had to dree –
Upon the partner of his waes
  He often turn'd a pitying e'e.

His bosom raise, he cou'dna speak'
  Her lot he inly did bemoan;
How sunk the e'e, and pale the cheek,
  Where once the beams of beauty shone.

That day she made the bridal vow,
  How bright she beam'd in youthfu' charms;
Yet Edwin thought her lovelier now,
  With ragged infants in her arms.

His bosom own'd nae selfish smart,
  His part o' waes he weel could bear;
But ah, these objects wrung his heart
  Their mis'ry made them doubly dear.

Indulgent heaven hath hid from man
  The fortune of the future day –
Was that pourtray'd within his scan,
  What would he gain but sad dismay!

To gaze upon the distant part,
  Would constitute a drear employ;
The dreams of hope would leave the heart,
  And dash each transient gleam of joy.

The darksome night was closing fast,
  A tempest dimm'd each twinkling star;
The wand'rers sought to shun the blast
  Beneath a mined impending scaur.

The fibres of the tangled thorn,
  Thick o'er their heads fantastic hang;
They there resolved to wait the morn,
  That night nae farther could they gang.

In this mansion, dark and drear,
  Darkess veil'd the mournful scene;
The shiv'ring infants quaked with fear,
  Till sleep in kindness closed their e'en.

O'er them hung the pensive pair,
  Slow the mournful mother crept;
For them breathed a parent's prayer,
  And kiss'd them softly as they slept.

Fast to her heart the pulses sped,
  Fondling oe'er these pledges dear;
Stretch'd them on their flinty bed,
  And o'er them dropt a mother's tear.

In their bosoms worn and faint,
  They found the beams of hope arise,
When they has pour'd their ardent plaint
  Before the Ruler of the skies.

Unto the plaintive cry of grief,
  He ne'er disdains his ear to bend;
With him the wretched find relief,
  And friendless virtue finds a friend.

More favour from celestial powers,
  Receives the lowly humble cell,
Than vaulted roofs and stately towers,
  Where gilded vice and folly dwell.

Though pent in misery's squalid vale,
  Like wretched outcasts of the earth,
Celestial solace ne'er will fail,
  To sooth the woes of suff'ring worth.

From innocence all pleasure flows,
  When every earthly bliss is flown;
In rags it yields more sweet repose,
  Than guilt can give on heaps of down.

When Edwin, free from care and pain,
  Wrapt in silkin slumbers lay,
The cavern, soak'd with sapping rain,
  At once the faithless roof gave way!

Whelming in the dismal cell,
   The sire, his children, and his wife;
Quick the pond'rous masses fell,
   And dash'd the feeble sparks of life.

Pale misery scarce deserves a sigh,
   On earth so transient in its sway,
And wealth and grandeur no envy,
   Those fleeting phantoms of a day.

See Edwin at the evening's close,
   Homeless, void of earthly things;
But when the morning sun arose,
On equal terms with breathless kings.

At the decisive hour of fate,
   Nor pomp nor splendour can avail;
The prince and peasant, poor or great,
   As vice or virtue turns the scale.

CAMERON'S ADDRESS TO HIS CLAN

Air: *Jamie's come Hame.*

Descendents of heroes! Whose fame knew no blots,
The pride of your country, the last of the Scots!
The morning's advancing, the lark's on the wing,
This day maun determine if Jamie is king.

Your injured country your pity implores,
The wrongs of your monarch sit on your claymores;
We on the proud foemen vengeance will bring,
And show these usurpers that Jamie's a king.

We proudly did own him when he was in power,
Nor will we forsake him when fortune looks sour;
We'll rather lie round him in cauld bloody ring,
And show them what Camerons dare do for their king.

See, Lochiel's banner stands proud in the line,
Oft it has waved o'er your brave fathers and mine,
Whose undaunted courage nae dangers cou'd ding.
O'er red heaps of ruin they follow'd their king.

Nor will we, their offspring, disgrace the proud line,
Nor tarnish the trophies that round it entwine;
Your blood and your chieftains doth claim the same spring,
Just fight like your fathers, and Jamie's a king.

Our foes are in motion, their horse comes in sight,
Perhaps they may need them, theyre useful in flight –
Now bagpipes and bugles, in rival notes sing,
Your honour, your country, and Jamie your king!

THE MOUNTAINS OF SPAIN

Air: *Humours of Glen*

Sweet balmy peace her soft way is extending,
   With gladness the march-beaten sogers return;
With hearts light and cheerful their way homeward
      bending;
   Back to their dear country, pale, weary and worn –
Day after day I impatiently languish'd
   To meet with my Billy – but now that's in vain;
The last rays of hope in my bosom's extinguish'd,
   For cold lies my love on the mountains of Spain.

The last happy hour that I pass'd with my Billy,
   Was where yon lone hawthorn stands low in the vale;
In beauty's full bloom was the primrose and lily,
   Sweet sang the mavis, and soft sigh'd the gale:
In that hour of anguish, when with him I parted,
   My beating heart hinted we'd ne'er meet again;
The chill pangs of anguish through my bosom darted,
   And cold ran my blood when he sailed for Spain.

Though the fields do look gay with the flowers in full
      blossom,
   Amidst all the beauties of nature I pine;
Each sweet little songster but wounds my sad bosom,
   It sings to its true love, and minds me of mine! –
When in broken slumbers I sink on my pillow,
   My woes, unextinguish'd, bewilder my brain,
In wild wand'ring fancy I cross the green billow,
And sit by his grave on the mountains of Spain.

The sons of ambition doth gloss a false story,
    To kindle young heroes in glory's career;
Pointing to fame in the proud path of glory,
    That phantom by many is purchased too dear!
O! had I been there when my Billy was dying,
    I'd fearlessly sought him 'mid heaps of the slain;
Aloft in my arms I had raised him when lying,
    And soothed his last sigh on the mountains of Spain.

A GLOSSARY OF
ROBERT DAVIDSON'S VOCABULARY

(Thanks are due to Chris Robinson, Director of the Scottish Language Dictionaries, for her invaluable assistance in the preparation of this glossary. Those interested in exploring further the meanings of these old Scots words should access the Scottish Language Dictionaries website at: www.dsl.ac.uk)

Aver	Old horse
Batie	Hare
Baudrons	Domestic cat
Crummy	Cow with a *crumpled* horn
Cuddy	Donkcy
Hawkie	Pet cow/whitefaced cow
Laverock	Skylark
Lintie	Linnet
Maukin	Hare
Paitrick	Partridge
Tod	Fox
Towmont	Wether/ two year old sheep

Airt	Direction
Alunt	Alight
Amous	Fondest, favourite
Athwart	Across
Ayont	Beyond

Bent/Bentie	Grass
Bield	Shelter
Bodle	Small coin of little value
Bogle	Ghost

Bowies	Barrels for holding ale
Buskit	Clad
Canty	Lively, pleasant
Callant	Young man
Carl	Man (derogatory term)
Carlin	Woman (derogatory term)
Chiel	Young man
Chitterin'	Chattering
Clautin	Scraping
Cour	Cower
Crouse	Confident, courageous
Crummy	Bent, twisted
Daurna	Dare not
Dowie	Sad, dismal
Dree	Suffer
Drumlie	Cloudy, discoloured, muddy, troubled (as in water)
Eikit	Added
Fend	Defence
Fittie	Whim
Fleg	Severe blow, kick
Forfauchin	Exhausted
Gangrel	Wandering
Gatherers	Gleaners (as in Biblical times) who, being the poor, were allowed to pick up from the field what little they could for themselves once the harvest was gathered in.
Gear	Personal property (including livestock)
Glebe	The Minister's field

Gonyels	Fools
Graithing	Making ready
Gowk	Cuckoo
Gowkship	Lordship (satirical)
Groat	Small coin of little value
Gauger	Exciseman
Guidman/Guidwife	Head of the Household/Mistress of the household
Haffets	Sidelocks/sidewhiskers (see *Lyart haffets* & *Lyart pow* i.e. silvery-whiskered & silver-headed)
Hafflins	Half
Hairst	Harvest
Heuks	Sickles, (not scythes) for cutting grain
Hind	Ploughman
Hirplin'	Limping
Ilk ane	Each one
Ingle	Hearth, fireside
Jouk	Dodge
Kent	Stick, long staff or pole
Kelpie	Water spirit (usually malignant & in the shape or form of a horse)
Kipel'd	Coupled, joined
Langsyne	Long ago
Lave	Wash
Leal	Faithful
Loof	Palm of hand or sole of foot

Lour	Threaten
Lyart	Silver-streaked (see *Haffets* and *Pow*)
Nieve	Fist
Nub	Club foot
Pelf	Worldly goods, profit
Plack	Small coin of little value
Pow	Head (see *Lyart Pow*, silver-haired)
Preen	Pin
Puirtith/poortith	Poverty
Roose	Praise
Rive	Tear or rip apart
Rung	Stick or cudgel
Shed	Small cottage, cot or hovel
Sinder'd	Sundered, parted
Skaith	Damage or hurt
Skelp	Slap or strike
Sklentin	Slanting (*The Term Day*). Deceiving (*The Gypsy's Rant*)
Souter	Shoemaker
Southron	Southern, English
Steekit	Shut
Stound	Stab of pain
Splore	Quarrel
Slae	Sloe berry
Speel'd	Climbed
Synd	A wash
Synde	To wash
Tentie	Attentive, watchful
Tither	Other
Towmond	Twelvemonth

Unco'	Extraordinary
Vap'rin'	Vapouring, boasting
Wabster/webster	Weaver
Wale	Best, pick
Warsal /warsling	Contend, struggle
Wight	Person
Wight	Spiritually strong
Yestreen	Yesterday (evening)

"At her hap"	At her predicament.
"At the ca"	At the *call* for the return to work (after a break)
"Burniewin' had kept the stoup a-steering"	The whisky flowed freely
"But & Ben"	Two-roomed cottage
"Change house"	An inn (where post or change horses were available to the traveller)
"Clautin at their coggies"	Scraping their bowls: enthusiastically eating & drinking
"Claw the Thairm"	To play the fiddle (i.e. to draw the bow across the *thairms* or animal guts from which the strings of the fiddle were made.
"The drudging bike"	The workaday world (by contrast with the carefree world of the non-working Gypsy)

217

"The blindness o' the bike"	*Bike* as in wasp *bink* or hive. The drones or worker bees seeing & knowing nothing but their work
Dung diled wi' her cantrips"	Entranced by her spells
"Egypt's auld bouricks"	Egypt's pyramids
"Hurkle down"	To crouch down
"If their fob is toom"	If their pockets are empty, if they don't pay up
"In a steer"	Stirred up, disordered
"Jeddart is their doom"	Taken for trial to Jedburgh Sheriff Court. 'Jeddart Justice' being notoriously swift and arbitrary: "In the morn they hang and draw, and sit in judgement after".
"Jim Crow"	*"Wheel about & turn about an do jus so. Ebry time I turn about I jump Jim Crow".* **1843 Virginia Minstrels Song.**
"John Barleycorn"	Whisky
"Pipe & mill"	Tobacco & snuff
"Reekin coggies"	Foaming beer mugs
"Rins redwood and shores them wi' the law"	Goes completely mad & threatens them with the law
"Tae gain the gree they ettle"	They strive for the prize
"The Land o' Cakes"	Scotland (i.e. the land of *oat* cakes)
"Thrang delvin"	Hard digging

"Getherin shelvie shuds"	*Shelves* or pieces of sheet ice which break loose, which get washed away & which lodge, *gather*, pile up and *shunt* over under each other in the awkward bends and corners of a river or stream once a thaw sets in.